The A to Z of
Foreign Musical Terms

FROM *ADAGIO* TO *ZIERLICH*

**A DICTIONARY FOR
PERFORMERS AND STUDENTS**

*The English equivalents of 3,000 foreign
expression marks and directions from French, German, Italian,
Latin, Portuguese and Spanish scores*

by

Christine Ammer

ECS Publishing

Boston, Massachusetts

The first edition of this book was published in 1971 under the title *Musician's Handbook of Foreign Terms*.

CONTENTS

ABBREVIATIONS

Brit.	British usage
cap.	capitalized
e.g.	for example
F.	French
G.	German
It.	Italian
L.	Latin
pl.	plural
Port.	Portuguese
Sp.	Spanish

AUTHOR'S NOTE

Virtually all of the terms in this book appear in actual musical scores. The main exceptions are organ stops, and pitch names and names of instruments in the four principal languages (French, German, Italian, Spanish). The terms are listed in strict alphabetical order, letter by letter, up to the comma in the case of inversion.   In the case of adjectives, both masculine and feminine forms are given whenever the two are very different or when both are frequently used.   When a single term has two or more entirely different meanings, such as *amaramente*, the reader is asked to rely on the context in which the term appears (that is, the style of the score) in order to determine which meaning is intended.

The terms in this book are drawn from more than 30,000 scores. Their original compilation was greatly assisted by Diana Cole, whose patient and conscientious research formed the basis of the first edition. The present book has been completely revised and expanded by the author.

A

a (1) (It.) To, from, by. For terms beginning with **a**, such as *a due*, see under second word. (2) (Sp.) To, at, in, by, of.

à (F.) To, at, in. For terms beginning with **à**, such as *à deux*, see under second word.

ab (G.) Off, meaning organ stops or mutes.

abafando (Port.) Muffled, muted.

abandon, avec (F.) Free, unrestrained, passionate. Also, **abandonné**.

abandono, con (Sp.) (1) Forlorn, yielding. Also, **con abandonamiento**. (2) Unrestrained, passionate.

abbandono, con (It.) Unrestrained, free, passionate.

abbastanza (It.) Enough, rather, e.g., *abbastanza lento*, rather slow.

abbruciante (It.) Fiery.

abdämpfen (G.) To mute (timpani, etc.).

aber (G.) But, e.g., *eilend aber leise*, fast but soft.

abgemessen (G.) In strict time.

abgestossen (G.) Same as DÉTACHÉ.

abnehmend (G.) Diminishing in loudness.

abschwellen (G.) Becoming softer.

absetzen (G.) To separate, either notes or phrases.

abstossen (G.) (1) In violin music, same as DÉTACHÉ. (2) In organ music, to take off a stop.

Abstrich (G.) Down-bow.

abstürzend (G.) Dropping sharply, suddenly softer.

abwechseln (G.) To alternate.

accablement, avec (F.) Heavily, very dejected.

a cappella (It.) See CAPPELLA.

accalorandosi (It.) Becoming excited, growing more animated.

accanito (It.) Also, **accanitamente**. (1) Frenzied, furious. (2) Persistent, obstinate.

accarezzevole (It.) Caressing, soothing, affectionate.

accelerando (It.) Becoming faster. Also, **accel.**

accélérant (F.) Becoming faster. Also, **accélérez**.

accent (F.) Expression, e.g., *d'un accent sauvage*, with fierce expression.

accentato (It.) Accented, emphasized, stressed. Also, accentuare, accentuato, con accentuazione.

accentué (F.) Accented, marked, stressed.

acceso (It.) Sparkling, brilliant.

acciaccatura (It.) A short grace note.

acciaccato (It.) Pounded, hammered.

accompagnando (It.) Accompanying.

accompagnant, en (F.) Accompanying.

accorato (It.) Sad, melacholy.

accordando, come (It.) As if in unison.

accordez sur (F.) Tune to.

accordo (It.) Chord, e.g., *tenuti gli accordi*, sustain the chords.

accordo d' (It.) In tune.

accouplé (F.) Coupler, ie., using a coupler. Also, accouplez.

accusé (F.) With emphasis.

acelerando (Sp.) Becoming faster. Also, acelerar.

acentuado (Sp.) Emphasized, stressed, accented. Also, acentuando.

Achtel (G.) Eighth note, eighth rest.

acusado (Sp.) Attacked.

acuta (It., L.) In organs, a mixture stop that includes a rank of pipes sounding a third higher than the keys played. Also, (L.) vox acuta.

acuto (It.) (1) High-pitched, shrill. (2) Sharp. (3) Top note.

adagietto (It.) A tempo somewhat faster than ADAGIO.

adagio (It.) A slow tempo, slower than ANDANTE but not as slow as LENTO.

addolcito (It.) Softer, sometimes also slower. Also, addolcendo.

adirato (It.) Enraged, angry.

ad libitum (L.) Freely, at will, improvised, meaning one may vary the tempo, perform or omit certain notes, voices, or parts, and/or add new notes, voices or parts.

adoucissant (F.) Becoming gentler and smoother.

aeolina (L.) In organs, a rank of very soft 8-foot string or foundation pipes tuned either slightly sharp or slightly flat.

aeoline (F.) In organs, one of the softest string stops.

aeoline céleste (F.) A very soft, undulating organ stop, made up of two ranks of aeoline pipes, one tuned normally and the other slightly sharp.

Aequalprinzipal (G.) In organs, the major 8-foot diapason or principal stop.

aereo (It.) Light, graceful, airy.

aérien (F.) Light, airy.

afectuoso (Sp.) Fondly, with warmth.

affabile (It.) Gentle, pleasing, graceful.

affaiblissez (F.) Become softer and weaker. Also, **affaibli.**

affannato (It.) Breathless, hurried, agitated. Also, **affannoso, affannosamente, con affanno.**

affectueusement (F.) Fondly, tenderly.

Affekt, mit (G.) Passionately. Also, **mit Affect.**

affetuoso (It.) Tenderly, with feeling. Also, **con affetto.**

affezione, con (It.) Tenderly, with feeling.

affirmatif (F.) Assertive, definite. Also, **affirmé.**

affolé (F.) Distracted, bewitched, maddened.

affrettando (It.) Hurrying, rushed, pressing on. Also, **affrettare, affrettato.**

afinar (Sp.) To tune.

agevole (It.) Easy, smooth, fluent.

aggizunione (It.) Same as NACHSCHLAG.

aggressivo (It.) Bold, forthright.

agiatamente (It.) With ease, unhurried, comfortably.

agíl (Sp.) Nimble, fast, light.

agilità, con (It.) Nimbly, lightly. Also, **agilmente.**

agitato (It.) Excited, restless. Also, **agitando, agitare, con agitazione.**

agité (F.) Excited, restless, fluttering.

agressivement (F.) Forthright, bold.

aigre (F.) Harsh, shrill.

aigu (F.) Sharp, shrill.

ailé (F.) Rapid and light, skimming.

ainsi que (F.) In the same way as, e.g., *ainsi qu'une flûte*, like a flute.

air, à l' (F.) In the air, up, e.g., *pavillon à l'air*, bell (of horn, etc.) pointed up.

airoso (Sp.) Graceful, light, lively.

Ais (G.) A-sharp.

aise, à l' (F.) Comfortably, easily.

Aisis (G.) A-double-sharp.

ajoutez (F.) Add, interpolate, e.g., add an organ stop.

Akkord (G.) Chord..

Akzent (G.) Accent.

akzentuiert (G.) Accented, emphasized, marked.

al (It.) To the.

alangui (F.) Slowed down, weaker, softer. Also, **en alanguissant.**

alato (It.) Eloquent, lofty.

a la vez (Sp.) At the same time.

a la vez que (Sp.) While.

alcuna (It.) Some, certain.

aleggiare (It.) Fluttering, quivering.

alegre (Sp.) Cheerful, gay. Also, **con alegría.**

alejándose (Sp.) Dying away, becoming distant.

alenti (F.) Slowed down.

alerte (F.) Lively, brisk.

algo (Sp.) Somewhat.

all°, allo. (It.) Short for ALLEGRETTO.

all', alla, alle, allo (It.) To the.

allant (F.) Lively, bustling.

allant, en (F.) Departing, vanishing.

allargando (It.) Slowing down, becoming broader and sometimes also louder.

alle (G.) All.

allegramente (It.) Cheerfully, gaily.

allègre (F.) Lively, sprightly, gay.

allegrettino (It.) A little ALLEGRETTO.

allegretto (It.) A moderately quick tempo, slower than ALLEGRO but faster than ANDANTE.

allegrissimo (It.) Very lively, a fast ALLEGRO.

allegro (It.) A fast, lively tempo, faster than ALLEGRETTO but slower than PRESTO.

allein (G.) Alone, only.

allentando (It.) Slowing down, slackening the tempo.

allez (F.) Go on, proceed.

allmählich (G.) Gradually. Also, **allmählig.**

allonger (F.) To slow down, to hold back, to delay.

allontandosi (It.) Withdrawing, dying away.

all^tto (It.) Short for ALLEGRETTO.

alma, con (1) (It.) With spirit, soulfully. (2) (Sp.) With vigor.

almeno (It.) At least, as much as.

alourdissez (F.) Make dull and heavy, weigh down. Also, **alourdir.**

al rovescio (It.) In reverse, meaning to play by retrograde motion or by inversion.

als (G.) As.

al seg. (It.) Short for al SEGNO.

als möglich (G.) As possible, e.g., *so schnell als möglich,* as fast as possible.

Alt (G.) Alto voice or part.

alterezza, con (It.) Haughtily, in a stately manner.

altissimo (It.) Highest (tuning). Also, **in altiss.**

alto (F.) Viola.

altre, le (It.) The others (than the soloist). Also, **gli altri.**

alzando (It.) Rising, becoming louder.

am (G.) By the, on the, e.g., *am Steg,* on the bridge.

amabile (It.) Tender, gentle. Also, **con amabilità.**

amaramente (It.) Also, **con amarezza.** (1) Harshly, sharply. (2) Sadly, painfully.

amer, amère (F.) Harsh, bitter.

amore con (It.) Fondly, with love, with warm feeling. Also, **amorevole, amoroso, amorosamente.**

amorosa (It.) In organs, a hybrid flute stop. Also, **flauto amabile.**

ampiamente (It.) Broadly. Also, **ampio, con ampiezza.**

ample (F.) Broadly, with dignity. Also, **amplement, avec ampleur.**

amplio (Sp.) Broad, full. Also, **ampliamente.**

an (G.) In organ music, draw a stop.

anacrouse (F.) Upbeat.

analoge (G.) Analogous, same.

anbetend (G.) Worshipful, adoring.

anche (It.) Also, as well.

anches (F.) (1) Reeds. (2) The reed instrument section of an orchestra. (3) The reed stops of an organ.

anchura, con (Sp.) (1) Broadly, fully. (2) Comfortably, easily.

ancora (It.) Again, still, e.g., *ancora più forte*, still louder.

Andacht, mit (G.) With devotion, prayerfully. Also, **andächtig.**

andante (It.) A moderately slow tempo, faster than ADAGIO but slower than ALLEGRETTO.

andantino (It.) Usually, a tempo slightly faster than ANDANTE but slower than ALLEGRETTO (but occasionally, slightly slower than andante is meant).

and^te (It.) Short for ANDANTE.

Anfang, vom (G.) From the beginning.

Anfangstempo (G.) Opening tempo. Also, **Anfangszeitmass.**

angemessen (G.) Comfortable, appropriate, in keeping with.

angenehm (G.) Pleasant, comfortable.

angeschlagen (G.) Also, **anschlagen.** (1) Struck, sounded. (2) Touched (strings or keys).

angoisse, avec (F.) With anguish, in a distressed manner. Also, **angoissé.**

angoscia, con (It.) Sorrowful, grieving, anguished. Also, **angoscioso.**

ängstlich (G.) Hesitantly, nervously.

anhalten (G.) To hold; same as FERMATA.

anhaltend (G.) Constant, continuous, e.g., *anhaltend laut*, constantly loud.

ánima, con (Sp.) Soulful, with feeling.

animación, con Sp.) Lively, bustling.

animado (Sp.) Lively.

animando (It.) Becoming lively and faster.

animato (It.) Lively, animated, spirited. Also, **con anima.**

animé (F.) Lively, animated. Also, **en animant, animez.**

anmutig (G.) Graceful. Also, **mit Anmut.**

anreissen (G.) In string playing, forceful attack.

ansante (It.) Breathless, panting, gasping.

anschlagen (G.) (1) To strike, to sound. (2) To touch (a key or string).

anschliessend, gleich (G.) Immediately adjoining, i.e., continue without pause.

anschwellend (G.) Becoming louder. Also, **anschwellen.**

ansiedad, con (Sp.) Anxiously, worriedly.

ansioso (It.) Eagerly, longingly, impatiently. Also, (It., Sp.) **con ansia.**

anstimmen (G.) (1) To tune. (2) To begin to sing.

anstürmend (G.) Rushing on.

antebrazo, con el (Sp.) With the forearm.

Anteil, mit (G.) In proportion, appropriately.

anterior (Sp.) Preceding, former, earlier, e.g., *ritmo anterior*, the preceding rhythm.

antes que (Sp.) Before, earlier than.

anticchiando (It.) (1) Humming. (2) Singing softly, pensively.

antwortend (G.) Answering. Also, **antworten.**

anwachsend (G.) Becoming louder.

apagado (Sp.) Softly, without emphasis, muffled, muted.

apaisé (F.) Calm, quiet. Also, **en s'apaisant.**

apasionado (Sp.) Impassioned.

à peine (F.) Hardly, scarcely.

aperto (It.) (1) Open, referring to open notes (horn), open pipes (organ). (2) Obvious, clear, e.g., *allegro aperto*, a definite allegro tempo. (3) In piano music, depress damper pedal.

Apfelregal (G.) In organs, an 8-foot regal stop.

a poco (Sp.) Immediately, soon, shortly.

apoyado (Sp.) With emphasis.

appassionato (It.) Passionate, ardent. Also, **appassionatamente.**

appena (It.) Scarcely, very slightly, e.g., *appena ritardando,* slowing down very slightly, *appena toccato,* scarcely played (i.e., very soft).

appesantendo (It.) Becoming heavier and broader.

appoggiando (It.) (1) Emphasized, reinforced. (2) Supporting, accompanying, e.g., *appoggiando il canto,* accompanying the melody (or vocal part).

appressando (It.) Approaching, coming closer, becoming louder.

appuntato (It.) Sharply, precisely.

appuyé (F.) With emphasis.

après (F.) After.

apresusar (Sp.) To hurry, press on.

âpreté, avec (F.) Harshly, violently. Also, **âpre.**

apurando (Sp.) Hurrying, pressing on.

arbitrio (It.) (Use)judgment,

(at one's) pleasure, e.g., *fare a proprio arbitrio,* perform as you wish.

arcata (It.) Bowing. Also, **arcata in giù,** down-bow; **arcata in su,** up-bow.

arcato (It.) Bowed.

archet (F.) Bow.

archi (It.) Stringed instruments.

arco (It.) (1)The bow, or use the bow. Also **coll'arco,** play with the bow. (2) Neck of a harp.

ardente (It.) Passionate, fervent, impetuous.

ardito (It.) Bold. Also, **arditamente.**

ardore, con (It.) With great warmth, fervently.

argentin (F.) Silvery, clear, bell-like.

argentino (It.) Same as ARGENTIN.

arioso (It.) (1) Melodic, singing. (2) An expressive vocal style.

armónicos (Sp.) Harmonics.

armonioso (It.) Tuneful, harmonious.

arpa (It., Sp.) Harp.

arpégé (F.) Like a broken chord (arpeggio). Also, **arpèges.**

arpeggiando (It.) Playing broken chords. Also, **arpeggiare.**

arpeggieren (G.) Same as ARPEGGIANDO.

arpeggio (It.) A broken chord (with notes played in succession instead of together).

arpegio (Sp.) Same as ARPEGGIO.

arraché (F.) (1) Forceful pizzicato. (2) Sharply accented.

arrastiando (Sp.) Dragging out, slow.

arrêt (F.) Stop, halt.

arrêtez (F.) Stop, e.g., *arrêtez l'archet*, stop bowing.

arrogamment (F.) Haughtily, proudly.

arrullo (Sp.) (1) Whispering, murmuring. (2) A lullaby.

articolando (It.) Pronouncing clearly and distinctly, articulating.

articulé (F.) Distinct, articulated.

-artig (G.) In the manner of,

like, e.g., *kadenzartig*, like a cadenza.

artig (G.) Neat, pleasing, polite. Also, **artiglich.**

As (G.) A-flat.

aspero (Sp.) Harsh, gruff.

aspro (It.) Harsh, rough, sharp. Also, **aspramente.**

assai (It.) Much, very, e.g., *allegro assai*, very fast.

assez (F.) Quite, enough, fairly, e.g., *assez vite*, fairly fast.

assombrissant, en s' (F.) Darkening, becoming gloomy.

assordire (It.) Deafening, very loud.

assorto (It.) Preoccupied.

astioso (It.) Envious, spiteful.

astuto (It.) Wide awake, bright, sharp.

ataque (Sp.) Attack.

Atem (G.) Breath.

atemlos (G.) Breathless.

a tempo (It.) See TEMPO, A.

attacca (It.) Continue without a pause. Also, **attacca subito.**

attaque (F.) Attack, touch.

attarder, s' (F.) To delay, to linger. Also, **attardé.**

attendre (F.) Wait, pause.

attendri (F.) Gently, tenderly.

atténué (F.) Weaker, softer.

au, aux (F.) At the, to the.

auch (G.) Also.

audacia, con (It.) Boldly.

auf (G.) (1) Open up, e.g., *Schalltrichter auf*, bells (of horns) up. (2) On, in, at, e.g., *auf* ♩= *66*, at (a tempo of) 66 half notes per minute; *Dämpfer auf*, with mutes.

aufbäumend (G.) Surging up, swelling.

auffahrend (G.) Passionate, vehement.

aufflackernd (G.) Flaring up, flickering, wavering.

aufflammend (G.) Flaring up.

aufgeblasen (G.) Arrogant, haughty.

aufgebracht (G.) Furious.

aufgeregt (G.) Excited, agitated.

aufhalten (G.) To hold back, to slow down.

aufjauchzend (G.) Shouting with joy.

auflebend (G.) Reviving, becoming livelier.

aufrauschend (G.) Swelling, becoming louder.

aufschluchzend (G.) Sobbing.

aufschreiend (G.) Crying out, shrieking.

Aufschwung (G.) With enthusiasm, soaring.

Aufstrich (G.) Up-bow.

Auftakt (G.) Upbeat.

Auftritt (G.) Scene.

Aufzug (G.) Act (of an opera).

augmentant, en (F.) Becoming louder. Also, **augmenter.**

aumentando (It., Sp.) Becoming louder.

aún (Sp.) Yet, still.

aus (G.) Out of.

ausbrechend (G.) Bursting out, explosive.

ausbreiten (G.) Becoming broader.

Ausdruck, mit (G.) With expression. Also, **ausdrucksvoll.**

ausdruckslos (G.) Without emphasis or expression, monotonous.

ausgeglichen (G.) Smooth, well-balanced, steady.

ausgelassen (G.) Exuberant, boisterous.

aushalten (G.) To sustain.

ausholen (G.) To attack.

ausklingen (G.) To die away.

ausladend (G.) Projecting, with a full tone.

auslaufen (G.) To conclude, to end.

Ausschwung (G.) Swing, momentum.

äusserst (G.) To the utmost, extremely, e.g., *äusserst ruhig*, as quiet as possible.

aussi bien que (F.) As well as.

aussingen (G.) To sing to the end.

aussi peu que (F.) As little as.

aussi – que possible (F.) As – as possible, e.g., *aussi doux que possible*, as soft as possible, *aussi fort que possible*, as loud as possible.

ausströmen (G.) To stream forth, to gush out.

austero (It.) Strict, severe, unadorned.

autant que (F.) As much as.

autoritaire (F.) Commanding, decisive.

autre (F.) Other. Also, **autres,** others (as opposed to soloist).

avant (F.) Before, in front of.

avantbras, avec l' (F.) With the forearm.

avanzar (Sp.) To push forward, to press on.

avec (F.) With.

avisée (F.) Prudent, careful.

avivar (Sp.) To speed up.

à volonté (F.) At will, freely, at the performer's discretion.

avvicinandosi (It.) Approaching.

avvilimento, con (It.) Dejected, discouraged humiliated. Also, **avvilito.**

avvivando (It.) Becoming livelier.

azione, con (It.) With action, staged.

B

B (G.) B-flat.

bacchantisch (G.) Reveling.

bacchetta (It.) (1) Drumstick, beater. Also, **bacch.** (2) Bowstick. (3) Baton; also, **bacchetta di direttore.**

badin (F.) Playful, droll.

badinant, en (F.) In fun, jestingly.

baguette (F.) (1) Baton. (2) Drumstick; also, **baguette de tambour.** (3) The stick of the bow.

baguette de timbale (F.) Kettledrum stick.

baigné de pédales (F.) Pedal throughout.

baixo (Port.) Bass.

baja, bajo (Sp.) Lower, e.g., *8a baja*, an octave lower.

bajón (Sp.) Bassoon.

balancé (F.) (1) Evenly. (2) A dance step.

baldanza, con (It.) Boldly, confidently.

ballabile (It.) Dancelike.

ballata, alla (It.) Dancelike.

ballmässig (G.) Dancelike.

ballo (It.) Dance, e.g., *tempo di ballo*, in dance tempo.

balzando (It.) Bouncy, springy.

barbaro (It.) Fierce, savage.

barcollante (It.) Tottering, staggering.

Bärpfeife (G.) In organs, a reed stop of the regal group.

Baryton (G.) In organs, a soft 8-foot reed stop.

basse (F.) Bass (part or voice), e.g., *la basse marquée*, the bass (part) emphasized.

Bassgeige (G.) Double bass.

Bassklarinette (G.) Bass clarinet.

basso (It.) Bass (part or voice), e.g., *basso marcato*, emphasize the bass (part).

basson (F.) Bassoon.

bastante (Sp.) Enough, rather, fairly, e.g., *bastante tranquilo*, rather calm.

batido (Sp.) Pounded, struck with force.

battement (F.) (1) Acoustical beats. (2) Formerly, an ornament.

---

battere (It.) (1) Beat a drum (or other percussion instrument). (2) Emphasize, stress insistently.

batteria (It.) Percussion section.

batterie (F.) Percussion section. (2) Drum roll.

battre (F.) To beat, to pant, to throb.

battre le mesure (F.) To beat time.

battuta (It.) (1) Measure, bar. (2) Beat, especially the accented first beat of a measure, e.g., *ritmo di tre battute*, a rhythm of three beats (one per measure).

battuta, a (It.) In strict time.

battuta d'aspetto (It.) One-measure rest.

battuta in aria (It.) Upbeat.

battuta in terra (It.) Downbeat.

battuto col legno (It.) Strike with the stick of the bow.

Bauernflöte (G.) In organs, a stopped wooden flute stop.

beaucoup (F.) Very, quite, much.

Becken (G.) Cymbals.

bedächtig (G.) Unhurried, deliberate.

bedeutend (G.) Considerably, definitely, e.g., *bedeutend laut*, quite loud.

bedrohlich (G.) Threatening, menacing.

Bedürfen, nach (G.) As one wishes (to perform).

Begeisterung, mit (G.) Enthusiastically, with spirit. Also, **begeistert.**

begleiten (G.) To accompany. Also, **Begleitung**, accompaniment.

behäbig (G.) Easily, comfortably.

behaglich (G.) Comfortably, with ease.

behende (G.) Nimbly, quickly.

behutsam (G.) Careful, wary, gingerly.

beide (G.) Both, e.g., *beide Pedal*, both pedals.

Beifall klatschend (G.) Applauding.

beinahe (G.) Almost, nearly.

beleben (G.) To revive, to animate.

belebt (G.) Brisk, animated. Also, **belebend.**

belebter (G.) Livelier.

Belieben, nach (G.) As one likes (to perform).

bellicoso (It.) Martial, brave. Also, **bellicosamente.**

belliqueux (F.) Martial.

bem (Port.) Well, thoroughly.

bemolle (It.) Flat, e.g., *A bemolle*, A-flat.

ben, bene (It.) Well, quite, e.g., *ben marcato*, quite accented, *ben ritmato*, quite rhythmic (with an even beat), *ben sentito*, warmly, enthusiastically.

bequem (G.) Comfortable, easy.

berceur (F.) Lullaby. Also, **berceuse.**

beruhigt (G.) Calm, quiet. Also, **beruhigend.**

beschaulich (G.) Meditative, quiet, tranquil.

beschleunigen (G.) To speed up, to increase the tempo. Also, **beschleunigt, beschleunigend.**

Beschluss (G.) End, conclusion.

beschwingt (G.) Light and swift, flying.

beschwörend (G.) Entreating, imploring.

beseelt (G.) Animated, lively.

besinnlich (G.) Thoughtful, reflective.

besorgt (G.) Anxious, disquieted. Also, **mit Besorgnis.**

bestiale (It.) Brutal, cruel.

bestimmt (G.) With decision.

betont (G.) Stressed, emphasized, accented. Also, **mit Betonung.**

Betonungen, ohne (G.) Without accents.

beträchtlich (G.) Considerably, a good deal.

bewegt (G.) Animated, with motion. Also, **mit Bewegung.**

bewegter (G.) Faster.

bianca (It.) Half note.

biecamente (It.) Grimly, sullenly.

bien (F.) Well, thoroughly.

bién (Sp.) Well, quite, very.

bis (1) (G.) Up to, until, e.g., *bis zum Schluss*, up to the end. (2) (L.) Twice, indicating a repeat.

bisbigliato (It.) Whispered. Also, **bisbigliando**, whispering.

biscroma (It.) Thirty-second note.

bisschen, ein (G.) A little, e.g., *ein bisschen schneller*, a little faster.

bissig (G.) Ferocious, biting, sharp.

bittend (G.) Pleading.

bizarre (F.) Strange, fanciful.

bizarro (It.) Unusual, fantastical, capricious. Also, **bizarramente**.

blanca (Sp.) Half note.

blanche (F.) Half note.

blandamente (It.) Gently, softly.

blando (Sp.) Tenderly, gently.
Blasinstrumente (G.) Wind instruments.

blass (G.) Colorless, pale, unemphasized, e.g., *mit blassem Ton*, with a colorless, flat tone.

Blechinstrumente (G.) Brass instruments. Also, **die Bleche**.

bleiben (G.) To stay, to remain, e.g., *im Tempo bleiben*, remain in strict time.

bleich (G.) Same as BLASS.

bloc chinois (F.) Chinese block.

Blockflöte (G.) (1) Recorder. (2) In organs, an open metal flute stop.

boca cerrada (Sp.) With the mouth closed, humming.

bocca chiusa, a (It.) Humming.

Bogen (G.) (1) Bow. (2) A tie or bind.

Bogenspitze, mit (G.) With the point of the bow.

bois (F.) (1) Wood, stick of the bow. (2) Woodwind instruments.

boîte (F.) In organs, the swell, e.g., *boîte fermée*, swell closed.

bombarde (F.) In organs, a powerful chorus reed stop.

bombarde quinte (F.) In organs, a chorus reed stop.

bombardino (Sp.) Euphonium.

bombardon (F.) In organs, a chorus reed stop.

bombastisch (G.) Inflated, conceited.

bombo (Sp.) Bass drum.

bon. (F.) Short for bassoon.

bonarietà, con (It.) With good nature, amiably.

bondissant (F.) Skipping, bounding.

bonheur, avec (F.) Happily.

bonté, avec (F.) Kindly, with good will.

borbottando (It.) Muttering, grumbling.

Bordunalflöte (G.) In organs, an open wooden flute stop. Also, **Portunalflöte.**

bouche (F.) Mouth.

bouché (F.) With stopping (in horns, etc.). Also, **bouchez.**

bouche fermée, à (F.) With closed mouth, humming.

bourdon (F.) (1) A bagpipe drone or sympathetic string. (2) Refrain. (3) In organs, an important stopped flute stop. Also, **bourd.** (4) The largest bell of a carillon.

Bourdonecho (F., G.) In organs, a very soft stopped flute stop. Also, **echo bourdon.**

bourrasque (F.) Angry, stormy.

bousculer (F.) To hurry, to become agitated. Also, **bousculade.**

Br. (G.) Short for viola.

Bratsche (G.) Viola.

Bravour, mit (G.) Brilliantly, with dash, with great skill.

bravoure, avec (F.) Bravely, gallantly.

bravura, con (It.) With great technical skill, in a virtuoso manner.

bref, brève (F.) Concise, brief.

breit (G.) (1) Broad, same as LARGO. (2) Broadly, e.g. *breit gestrichen*, broadly bowed.

breve (It.) Brief, concise; appearing over ⌒ , short pause. Also see BREVE, ALLA.

breve, alla (It.) (1) 2/2 meter *(cut time)*. (2) Twice as fast as before.

brilhante (Port.) Brilliant, sparkling.

brillant (F.) Brilliant, showy, sparkling.

brillante (It.) Sparkling, spirited.

brincando (Sp.) Skipping, bounding.

brindisi (It.) Drinking song.

brio, con (It.) Vigorously, with fire. Also, **brioso.**

brisé (F.) Short detached bow strokes.

brivido (It.) Shivering, trembling.

brouillé de pédale (F.) In organ playing, a mixture of pedal stops.

brumeux (F.) Misty, veiled.

brummen (G.) To hum. Also, **Brummstimme.**

brusca, brusco (Sp.) Roughly, harshly.

brusco (It.) Sharply, curtly, abruptly. Also, **bruscamente.**

brusque (It.) Sharp, abrupt, sudden. Also, **brusquement.**

brutale (It.) Savage, fierce, cruel.

bugle à pistons (F.) Flugelhorn.

buccina (1) (It.) In organs, a chorus reed stop. (2) (L.) Trumpet.

buffa, buffo (It.) Comic, clownish.

buio (It.) Dark.

burla, alla (It.) Playful, joking.

burlesco (It.) Jesting, light.

burlesk (G.) Mock-heroic.

C

caché (F.) Hidden, discreet, subtle.

cada (Sp.) Each, every.

cadencé (F.) (1) Measured, rhythmic. (2) Trilled.

cadendo (It.) Becoming softer.

cadenza (It.) (1) A cadenza, a brilliant, often florid solo, usually at the end of a movement or piece. (2) Cadence, close.

cadenzato (It.) In a regular rhythm, measured.

caesura (L.) Pause.

caisse (F.) Drum. Also **grosse caisse,** bass drum.

caisse claire (F.) Snare drum.

caisse roulante (F.) Tenor drum. Also, **caisse sourde.**

calando (It.) Becoming softer and slower.

calcando (It.) (1) Forcefully, pressing on. (2) Imitating, copying.

caldo (It.) Heated, passionate.

calmando (It.) Quieting down, subsiding. Also, **calmandosi, calmato.**

calmant, en se (F.) Becoming calm, tranquil. Also, **calmer, calmez.**

calme (F.) Tranquil, still, quiet.

calore, con (It.) With warmth, fervent, impetuous. Also, **caloroso.**

cambiare (It.) To change, meaning change instruments, crooks, mutes, etc.

caminando (Sp.) Same as CAMMINANDO.

camminando (It.) Moving on, flowing.

campana (It.) (1) Bell, chime. Also, **campane,** bells (orchestral) chimes. (2) The bell of a wind instrument, e.g., *campane in aria,* with the bells up. (3) In organs, a brilliant high flute or foundation stop. Also, **Zimbelflöte.**

campanas (Sp.) Chimes.

campanella (It.) Small bell. Also, **campanello,** pl. **campanelle, campanelli.**

campanette (It.) Glockenspiel. Also, **camp.**

canción (Sp.) Song.

candeur, avec (F.) Openly, ingenuously, simply.

cantabile (It.) In a singing style, lyrical, melodious, flowing. Also, **cant.,** (It., Sp.) **cantando.**

cantando (Sp.) (1) Same as CANTABILE. (2) Singing.

cantellerando (It.) Humming, singing softly.

canticchiando (It.) (1) Humming. (2) Singing softly.

cantilena (It.) (1) Lullaby. (2) Melodious. (3) A monotonous, singsong style of performance.

canto (It.) (1) Song. (2) Singing, vocal part. (3) Soprano (treble) part. (4) Melody.

capo (It.) Beginning, e.g., *da capo al fine,* from the beginning to the end, *da capo al segno* (𝄌), from the beginning to the sign. Also, part of the abbreviation D.C. (da capo).

cappella (It.) (1) A choir (singers or instrumentalists). (2) **a cappella,** unaccompanied voice(s). (3) **tempo a cappella,** same as BREVE, ALLA.

capriccioso (It.) Fanciful, freely. Also, **capricciosamente.**

caprichosamente (Port., Sp.) Fanciful, whimsical.

capricieux (F.) Fanciful, playful.

carattere, in (It.) In character, typical, appropriate.

caressant (F.) Tender, soothing.

carezzando (It.) Loving, affectionate. Also, **carezzoso.**

carezzevole (It.) Coaxing, caressing, wheedling.

caricato (It.) Heightened, intensified, exaggerated.

caricaturale (It.) Caricatured, over-exaggerated.

carillon (F.) (1) Glockenspiel. (2) In organs, a mixture stop. Also, **Glockenspiel.**

casi (Sp.) Almost, nearly, e.g., *casi f*, almost forte (loud).

cassa (It.) Drum. Also, **gran cassa**, bass drum.

cassa rullante (It.) Tenor drum.

castañuelas (Sp.) Castanets.

c.b. (F., It.) Short for contra-

bass (double bass).

cedendo (It.) Yielding, slowing down.

cédez (F.) Slow down and become softer. Also, **céder.**

cediendo (Sp.) Slowing down.

celere (It.) Swift, rapid.

céleste (F.) (1) Heavenly, divine, otherwordly. (2) In organs, an undulating beating stop, usually made up of two ranks of deliberately mistuned pipes, e.g., **dolce céleste, gemshorn céleste, gamba céleste,** etc. Also, see VOIX CÉLESTE.

celestina (It.) In organs, a very small-scaled open flute stop.

cembalo (G., It.) Harpsichord.

centro, al (It.) At the center (e.g., of a drum).

cercle, sur le (F.) At the rim (of a drum).

cerrado (Sp.) Closed, stopped.

Ces (G.) C-flat.

Ceses (G.) C-double-flat.

chaleur, avec (F.) With warmth, fervently. Also, **chaleureux.**

chalumeau (F.) (1) An obsolete form of clarinet. (2) The low register of modern clarinets. (3) In organs, same as SCHALMEI.

chamade (F.) In organs, same as TROMPETTE EN CHAMADE.

changez en (F.) Change to.

chant (F.) (1) Song. (2) Melody, theme. (3) Voice(s).

chantant (F.) In a singing, melodious style. Also, chanté.

chanterelle (F.) Highest string (in violins, etc.)

chaque (F.) Each, every.

charme, avec (F.) With charm, gracefully.

chatoyant (F.) Brilliant, showy.

chaud (F.) Warmly, with fervor.

chauffez (F.) Become faster, press on.

che (It.) That, which, than, e.g., *più forte che d'inizio,* louder than at the beginning.

cheto (It.) Quiet, hushed.

chevalet, au (F.) On the bridge (of violins, etc.).

cheville (F.) Tuning pin, tuning peg. Also, chev.

chevrotant (F.) Quivering, trembling.

chiaro (It.) Clear, bright, distinct. Also, chiaramente.

chiassoso (It.) Noisy, babbling, creating a din.

chiavi, con le (It.) Strike the keys only (woodwinds).

chitarra (It.) Guitar.

chiusa, chiuso (It.) Closed.

choeur (F.) Choir.

Chor (G.) Choir.

chrétiennement (F.) Charitably.

chuchoté (F.) Whispered.

cierta, cierto (Sp.) Certain, definite, positive.

cimbalo (It.) (1) Cymbal. (2) Harpsichord. (3) Tambourine.

címbalo (Sp.) Cymbal.

cinelli (It.) Cymbals.

cinglant (F.) Harsh, grating.

circa (It., L.) About, approximately, e.g., *circa* ♩ = *54,* at approximately (the tempo of) 54 quarter notes per minute.

Cis (G.) C-sharp.

Cisis (G.) C-double-sharp.

cistre (F.) Zither.

cl. (F., It.) Short for clarinet.

clair (F.) Clear, bright, distinct. Also, **clairement.**

clairon (F.) (1) Bugle. (2) In organs, a trumpet stop. Also, **clarion, trumpet clarion.**

clairon harmonique (F.) In organs, an octave chorus reed stop with a powerful tone. Also, **clarion harmonic, harmonic clarion.**

clarabella (It.) In organs, an open flute stop.

clarinete (Port., Sp.) Clarinet.

clarinette (F.) Clarinet.

clarinette basse (F.) Bass clarinet.

clarinetto (It.) Clarinet.

claro (Port., Sp.) Clear, distinct, pure.

clarone (It.) Bass clarinet. Also, **clarinetto basso.**

clavecin (F.) Harpsichord.

clavicembalo (It.) Harpsichord.

clavicordio (Sp.) Harpsichord.

clavier (F.) Keyboard, manual.

clignant de l'oeil (F.) Winking.

cloches (F.) Bells, chimes.

coda (It.) End, concluding passage.

col, colla, colle (It.) With the.

colère, avec (F.) Angrily, with passion, furiously.

colpo di lingua (It.) Tonguing.

com (Port.) With.

come (It.) How, like, as, e.g., *come un brivido*, like a shudder, *come prima*, like the first time, *come sopra*, as above, *come sta*, as written.

cómico (Sp.) Droll, humorous.

comienza (Sp.) Beginning, opening, e.g., *en el tempo de comienzo*, in the opening tempo.

comique (F.) Comical, humorous.

comme (F.) Like, as, as if.

commencer (F.) Begin, e.g., *commencer lentement*, begin slowly. Also, **commencez.**

commodément (F.) Easily, comfortably.

commosso (It.) Irritated, annoyed.

como (Sp.) As, like, in the manner of, e.g., *tan lento como sea pueda*, as slow as possible.

cómodante (Sp.) Comfortably, easily. Also, **cómodo.**

comodo (It.) Comfortable, easy, unhurried.

compasso (Port.) (1) Time, meter. (2) Measure, bar.

completo (It.) Wholly, entirely.

compter (F.) To count, e.g., *compter à la double-croche*, to count from (to) the sixteenth note.

con (It., Sp.) With, e.g., (It.) *con calore*, with fervor, *con sordini*, with mutes.

concentrando (It.) Concentrating, condensing, becoming faster.

concentré (F.) Concentrated, dense.

concertato (It.) (1) Soloists, especially those alternating with the full orchestra in a concerto grosso. Also, **concertino, concertante.** (2) Conducted. (3) Scored, orchestrated.

concitato (It.) Excited, agitated, usually in fast tempo. Also, **concitando, con concitazione.**

concluir (Sp.) To end, conclusion.

con esp. (It.) Short for **con espressione;** see ESPRESSIVO.

confus (F.) Vague, indistinct.

conserver (F.) Keep, retain, e.g., *conserver le rythme de marche*, retain march rhythm.

cont. (F., It.) Short for contrabassoon (double bassoon). Also, **cont.f., c.fag.**

contemplatif (F.) Same as CONTEMPLATIVO.

contemplativo (It.) Dreamy, meditative.

continu (F.) Continued, maintained. Also, **continué.**

continuo (It.) Continuous bass accompaniment, especially as found in baroque music. Also, **basso continuo.**

contrabajo (Sp.) Double bass, contrabass.

contrabajón (Sp.) Contrabassoon.

contrabasso (It.) Double bass.

contra bombarde (L. + F.) In organs, a deep-toned chorus reed stop.

contra bourdon (L. + F.) In organs, same as SOUBASSE.

contra dulciana (It.) In organs, a very soft foundation stop.

contrafagotto (It.) (1) Contra-bassoon. (2) In organs, a low-pitched reed stop.

contra gamba (It.) In organs, a low-pitched string stop. Also, **Grossgamba.**

Contra Posaune (G.) In organs, a low-pitched, loud chorus reed stop.

contra viola (It.) In organs, a string stop.

contra violone (It.) In organs, a bass string stop. Also, **bass violin, contre viole, double bass, violin bass, violone.**

contrebasse (F.) Double bass, contrabass.

contrebasse à pistons (F.) Bass tuba.

contrebasson (F.) Contra-bassoon.

contre viole (F.) In organs, same as CONTRA VIOLONE.

coperto (It.) Covered, muted.

copula (L.) In organs, a stop designed to blend the tones of other stops.

cor (F.) Horn, French horn.

cor. (It.) Short for horn(s).

corale (It.) (1) Choral, pertaining to a choir or its music. (2) Chorale (the musical form).

cor anglais (F.) (1) English horn. (2) In organs, an 8-foot reed stop whose tone resembles that of the orchestral English horn.

corchea (Sp.) Eighth note.

corda (It.) String, pl. **corde.** Also see TRE CORDE, UNA CORDA.

corde (1) (It.) Strings. (2) (F.) String, e.g., **pincer la corde,** pluck the string.

cor d'amour (F.) In organs, same as CORNO D'AMORE.

cor de basset (F.) In organs, same as CORNO DI BASSETTO.

cor de chasse (F.) In organs, same as WALDHORN.

cor de nuit (F.) In organs, same as NACHTHORN.

cornamusa (It.) Bagpipe.

cornemuse (F.) Bagpipe.

corneta (Sp.) Cornet.

cornet à bouquin (F.) Cornett.

cornet à pistons (F.) Cornet.

cornet de récit (F.) In organs, a compound stop of unusually prominent tone.

cornet des bombardes (F.) In organs, a compound stop made up of several ranks of loud, open diapason pipes.

cornet des violes (F.) In organs, a compound stop made up of several ranks of string pipes.

cornetta (It.) Cornet. Also, **cornetta a pistoni, pist.**

cornetto (It.) (1) Cornett. (2) Organ stop.

corno (It.) Horn, French horn. Also, pl. **corni.**

corno d'amore (It.) In organs, a solo reed stop. Also, **cor d'amour.**

corno di bassetto (It.) (1) Basset horn. (2) In organs, an 8-foot manual reed stop whose tone is similar to that of the basset horn. Also, **cor de basset.**

corno di caccia (It.) In organs, same as WALDHORN.

corno inglés (Sp.) English horn. Also, **cuerno inglés.**

corno inglese (It.) English horn. Also, **cor ingl., c.ingl.**

corona (It.) (1) Pause. (2) The sign for the fermata (⌢). Also, **lunga corona.**

corrente (It.) (1) Rapid, flowing. (2) A dance similar to the COURANTE.

correr (Sp.) Fast.

correre, senza (It.) Without hurrying.

corta, corto (It., Sp.) Short, brief, concise.

coulé (F.) A slide, similar to a GLISSANDO.

coulisse (F.) Slide (in wind instruments).

coup de vent, comme un (F.) Like a gust of wind, breathy.

courante (F.) (1) Running, rapid, flowing. (2) An old dance.

courroux (F.) Wrath, anger.

court (F.) Short, brief, concise.

crécelle (F.) Orchestral rattle.

crepitante (It.) Crackling, rustling.

crescendo (It.) Becoming louder, swelling. Also, **cresc., cres.**

crespo (It.) Rippling.

cri, comme un (F.) Like an outcry.

cristalino (Sp.) Clear, bright, transparent.

cristallin (F.) Clear, silvery.

cristallino (It.) Clear, bright, pure.

croche (F.) Eighth note.

croisez les mains (F.) Cross the hands. Also, en croisant.

croma (It.) Eighth note.

cromorne (F., It.) (1) In organs, same as KRUMMHORN. (2) The crumhorn (obsolete woodwind instrument).

crotchet (Brit.) Quarter note.

cuadro (Sp.) Four.

cuerda (Sp.) String (of violins, etc.) Also, cuerdas, strings, stringed instruments.

cuivre, en (F.) Of metal (mutes).

cuivrez (F.) Produce a forced, brassy tone. Also, cuivré.

cullando (It.) Rocking, soothing.

cupo (It.) Gloomy, deep, with a dark tone. Also, con voce cupa.

cymbales (F.) Cymbals.

D

d' (F., It.) Of.

da, dal, dalla, dalle, dall' (It.) From the, by the.

dämonisch (G.) Devilish, fiendish, wild.

Dämpfer (G.) Mute, e.g., mit Dämpfer (auf), with mute, Dämpfer weg (ab), without mute.

dans (F.) In.

dansant (F.) Dancing.

danza, como (Sp.) Dancelike.

das (G.) The.

Daumen (G.) Thumb.

davantage (F.) More, further.

D.C. (It.) Short for da CAPO.

de (F., Sp.) Of, from.

déaccouplé (F.) Uncoupled, separated.

debole (It.) Faint, weak. Also, debile.

début (F.) Beginning.

déchirant (F.) Heartrending, piercing.

décidé (F.) Firm, resolute.

decisivo (It.) Decisive, firm.

deciso (It.) Bold, forceful.

declamato (It.) Recited, spoken. Also, **declamando.**

declamé (F.) In a declamatory style.

decrescendo (It.) Becoming softer. Also, **decr., decresc.**

défaillant (F.) Giving way, feeble, dying away.

défi, avec (F.) With defiance, challenging.

degli (It.) Of the.

dehnen (G.) To broaden, to prolong.

dehors, en (F.) Emphasized, standing out, accented.

deixa (Port.) Let, allow, e.g., *deixa vibrar*, let (continue to) sound.

dejad (Sp.) Same as DEIXA. Also, **dejar.**

deklamieren (G.) (1) To recite. (2) To perform as a recitative.

del, dell', della, delle, dello (It.) Of the, than the.

deliberamente (It.) Deliberately, ponderously.

delicadeza, con (Sp.) With refinement, daintily, elegantly. Also, **delicado.**

delicadísimo (Sp.) Highly refined and elegant.

délicat (F.) Smoothly, delicately, daintily. Also, **délicatement.**

delicatamente (It.) Daintily, elegantly. Also, **delicato, con delicatezza.**

délices, avec (F.) With delight, happily.

delikat (G.) Delicate, tenderly.

delirando (It.) Raving, wild.

délire, en (F.) Frenzied.

delizia, con (It.) With pleasure, joyfully.

dem (G.) The.

demasiado (Sp.) Too much, excessive.

demi jeu (F.) The softer organ stops.

demi-pause (F.) Half rest.

demisemiquaver (Brit.) Thirty-second note.

demi-soupir (F.) Eighth rest.

demi-teinte, en (F.) Half-shaded, subtly shaded.

demi-voix, à (F.) Half-voice, softly.

demuthsvoll (G.) Humbly, modestly. Also, **demütig.**

den (G.) The.

dengoso (Sp.) Affected, over-refined.

de plus en plus (F.) More and more.

deprisa (Sp.) Depressed, pushed down.

der (G.) The.

derb (G.) Robust, rough.

derecha, derecho (Sp.) Right (hand).

derisione, con (It.) Mockingly.

dernier, derniére (F.) Last.

Des (G.) D-flat.

descendant (F.) Descending, e.g., *arpège descendant,* descending broken chord.

desconsolado (Sp.) Grief-stricken, downhearted.

desenfado, con (Sp.) Freely, easily.

Deses (G.) D-double-flat.

désespoir, avec (F.) Despairingly.

desfalleciendo (Sp.) Becoming softer, fading away.

desgarrado (Sp.) Shameless, bold.

desiderato (It.) Desired, welcome.

desiderio, con (It.) With yearning, longingly.

désinence (F.) Ending, final cadence.

desoladamente (Sp.) Sad, disconsolate.

desolato (It.) Sorrowful, disconsolate. Also, **con desolazione.**

désordonné (F.) Disorderly, confused.

despacio (Sp.) Slowly, deliberately.

dessus (F.) On, over, above, e.g., *main droit dessus,* right hand over (the left).

destacado (Sp.) Emphasized, standing out, accented. Also, **destacando.**

desto (It.) Agile, quick, sprightly.

destra (It.) Right (hand).

détaché (F.) In bowing, alternate up- and down-bows, either legato or detached.

detención (Sp.) Hold, stop, e.g., *detención todos juncos*, everyone stop together.

détendu (F.) Slackened, slower.

deutlich (G.) Clear, distinct.

deux (F.) Two.

devoto (It.) Dedicated, sincere. Also, **devotamente.**

dezent (G.) Restrained, dignified, moderate.

di (It.) Of, from, by, e.g., *in modo di ballo*, in the manner of a dance.

diapason (F.) In organs, a foundation stop that gives the instrument its characteristic tone.

diaphane (F.) Clear, transparent.

die (G.) The.

dièse (F.) Sharp, e.g., *F-dièse*, F-sharp.

diesis (It.) Sharp, e.g., *A-diesis*, A-sharp.

diffuso (It.) Blurry, scattered; the opposite of clear and concise.

dignitá, con (It.) With dignity, gravely.

dileguando (It.) Growing fainter and fainter.

diluendo (It.) Becoming weaker and softer, fading away.

dim (It.) Short for DIMINUENDO. Also, **dimin.**

diminuant, en (F.) Becoming softer.

diminuendo (It.) Becoming softer. Also, **dim., dimin.**

dinámica (Sp.) (1) Lively, vibrant. Also, **dynámico.** (2) Dynamics.

di nuovo (It.) Again, anew.

direita (Port.) Right (hand).

Dis (G.) D-sharp.

discrètement (F.) Cautiously, with reserve.

disinvolto (It.) Freely, easily, deftly.

Disis (G.) D-double-sharp.

disminyuendo (Sp.) Same as DIMINUENDO. Also, **disminuir.**

disparaissant, en (F.) Disappearing, fading away.

disperazione, con (It.) Wildly, despairingly, despondently. Also, disperatamente, **disperato.**

disprezzo, con (It.) Contemptuously, scornfully.

distaccato (It.) Detached, separated.

distanza, a (It.) In the distance, from afar, soft. Also, **distante, distantemente.**

disteso (It.) Extended, broad.

distinct (F.) Clear, distinct.

distinto (It.) Clear, distinct, separate.

div. (It.) Short for DIVISI.

diventando (It.) Becoming, changing to, e.g., *diventando allegro*, becoming fast.

divisés, en (F.) Same as DIVISI. Also, **par divisés.**

divisi (It.) Indicating separate parts where normally there is only one, e.g., the first violins dividing to play two or more separate parts. Also, **div.**

doigté (F.) Fingering.

do (F., It., Sp.) The note or key of C, e.g., (It.) *tromba in do*, C trumpet.

dolce (It.) (1) Sweet, smooth, gentle. Also, **dolciato, dol.** (2) In organs, a fairly soft foundation stop.

dolcissimo (It.) (1) As sweet and gentle as possible (see DOLCE). Also, **dolciss.** (2) In organs, a very soft foundation stop.

dolent (F.) Mournful, plaintive.

dolente (It.) Sorrowful, mournful.

doloroso (It.) Lamenting, grieving. Also, **con dolore.**

donaire (Sp.) Graceful, elegant. Also, **donairoso, donairosamente.**

dopo (It.) After, beyond, then.

Doppelflöte (G.) In organs, a stopped flute stop, with two mouths per pipe.

Doppelgedeckt (G.) In organs, a stopped flute stop, with two mouths per pipe.

Doppelgriff (G.) Double stop.

Doppelrohrflöte (G.) In organs, a half-covered flute stop.

Doppelrohrgedeckt (G.) In organs, a half-covered flute stop.

Doppelspitzflöte (G.) In organs, an open flute stop.

doppelt (G.) Twice as, double, e.g., *doppelt so schnell*, twice as fast, *doppelt so langsam*, twice as slow.

doppio (It.) Double, twofold, twice as, e.g., *doppio bemolle*, double flat, *doppio colpo di lingua*, double tonguing, *doppio movimento*, twice as fast, *doppio corda*, double stop.

dos (Sp.) Two, e.g., *dos pedales*, two pedals.

double, le (F.) (1) A repeat. (2) A variation. (3) A 16-foot organ stop.

double-croche (F.) Sixteenth note.

doublette (F.) In organs, a stop made up of two diapason ranks of different pitches.

douce, doux (F.) Soft, gentle, smooth. Also, **doucement, avec douceur.**

douloureux (F.) Sorrowful. Also, **douloureusement.**

Dpf. (G.) Short for mute(s).

dramático (Sp.) Dramatic, emotional.

drammatico (It.) Dramatically, somewhat exaggerated. Also, **drammaticamente, con dramma.**

drängend (G.) Pressing on, hurrying. Also, **drängen, mit Drang.**

dreitaktig (G.) Beat in three.

dreiteilig (G.) Three-part.

dringend (G.) Urgent, pressing.

drohend (G.) Threatening.

dröhnend (G.) Booming, resounding.

Druck (G.) Pressure, strain, e.g., *ohne jeden Druck*, without straining, easily.

D.S. (It.) Short for dal SEGNO.

du (F.) From the, of the.

due (It.) Two, e.g., *due volte*, two times (twice).

due, a (It.) (1) Two together. Also, **a 2.** (2) For two (parts).

due, in (It.) (1) In two parts. (2) With two beats.

due corde (It.) (1) Release soft (*una corda*) pedal. (2) Play note on two strings (violin, etc.).

duetto (It.) Duet.

duftig (G.) Sweetly, light.

dulce (Sp.) Sweet, smooth, gentle. Also, **dulcemente.**

dulciana (It.) In organs, a soft stop similar to the diapasons in quality. Also, **echo diapason.**

Dulzian (G.) In organs, an important reed stop. Also, **dulcian.**

dumpf (G.) (1) Dull, hollow, muffled. (2) Depressed, gloomy.

dünn (G.) Thin, delicate, tenuous.

duolo, con (It.) Grieving, sorrowful.

dur (1) (F.) Harsh, rough. Also, **dure, avec dureté.** (2) (G.) Major, e.g., *A-dur*, A major.

duramente (It.) Harshly, severely. Also, **duro, con durezza.**

durchdringen (G.) Pressing through, emerging.

durchaus (G.) Throughout.

durchsichtig (G.) Transparent, very clear.

durchweg (G.) Consistently, throughout.

duro (It., Sp.) Harsh, rough.

düster (G.) Dark, gloomy, sad.

dynamique (F.) Energetic, vigorous.

E

e (It.) (1) And. (2) Is.

ebbrezza, con (It.) With elation, enraptured, blissful.

eben so (G.) Just as, equally, e.g., *eben so schnell*, just as fast.

éblouissant (F.) Dazzling.

ebollimento (It.) A sudden outburst of feeling.

eccitando (It.) Becoming excited or agitated. Also, **eccitato.**

echo (G., etc.) In organs, name for various soft stops, such as **echo diapason, echo dulciana, echo gemshorn,** etc.

écho, en (F.) Echoing.

echotonartig (G.) Echolike.

éclat, avec (F.) With a sudden burst.

éclatant (F.) (1) Brilliant, sparkling. (2) Piercing, shrill.

eco (It.) Echo, an echo effect.

écroulez (F.) Crash down.

ed (It.) And.

effaçant, en s' (F.) Fading away, becoming fainter.

effacé (F.) Suppressed, kept in the background.

effetto, con (It.) Dramatically, forcefully.

effleurant, en (F.) Touching lightly, skimming over.

effleuré (F.) Very light, gliding.

effondrement (F.) Deep-delving.

effusione, con (It.) Pouring out, emotional.

égal (F.) Equal (in duration, time value, etc.), even, regular. Also, (pl.) égaux, e.g., les triolets égaux, equal triplets.

également (F.) Uniformly.

eguale (It.) Even, smooth. Also, egualmente, eguabilmente.

eigensinnig (G.) Headstrong, unyielding.

eigenwillig (G.) Willful, stubborn.

eilend (G.) Hurrying, rapid. Also, eilen, mit Eile.

eilfertig (G.) Hasty, speedy, headlong. Also, eilig.

ein (G.) One, a, an. Also, eine, eins.

eindringlich (G.) Pressing, urgent.

einfach (G.) (1) Simple, plain. (2) Single (not doubled).

Einleitung (G.) Introduction. Also, einleiten, to introduce.

einlenkend (G.) Relenting, yielding.

einmal (G.) Once.

Einsatz (G.) Attack, entrance. einsetzend (G.) (1) Inserting, interpolating. (2) Installing, establishing.

ein wenig (G.) A little, e.g., ein wenig schneller, a little faster.

Eis (G.) E-sharp.

ekstatisch (G.) Rapturous, ecstatic.

el (Sp.) The.

élan, avec (F.) Bursting out, with dash, vehemently.

élargir (F.) Broaden and slow down. Also, en élargissant, élargi, elargissez, élargissement.

elasticito (It.) Springy, bouncy. Also, con elasticità.

elastisch (G.) Springy, bouncy, supple.

élégance, avec (F.) With grace and polish.

elegancia, con (Sp.) With elegance, with grace.

elegante (It.) Graceful, polished. Also, **elegantamente, con eleganza.**

elegaico (It.) Mournful, lamenting.

elevazione, con (It.) Lofty, noble. Also, **elevato.**

éloignant, en s' (F.) Becoming more distant, fading away. Also, **éloignez.**

eloquenza, con (It.) With eloquence, movingly. Also, **eloquente, eloquentemente.**

emergendo (It.) Becoming distinct, with gradually increasing emphasis. Also, **emergente.**

émouvant (F.) Moving, agitated.

empezar (Sp.) To begin, e.g., *empezar lentamente*, begin slowly.

Empfindung, mit (G.) With feeling, sensitivity, tenderly. Also, **empfindsam.**

emphase (F., G.cap.) Emphasis, stress.

emporté (F.) Fiery, passionate.

empressé (F.) Hurrying, rapid.

empujado (Sp.) Up-bow.

ému (F.) With feeling.

en (1) (F.) In. (2) (Sp.) In, at, on, e.g., *en tempo*, in strict time. For terms beginning with **en**, see second word.

encalçando (Port) Following closely.

enchaînez (F.) Connect, go on directly, LEGATO. Also, **enchaîner.**

enchantement, en (F.) Entranced, delighted.

enclumes (F.) Anvil.

encore (F.) Again, once more, still, e.g., *encore plus vite*, still faster.

energico (It.) With vigor, powerfully. Also, **con energia.**

énergique (F.) Vigorous, forceful. Also, **avec énergie.**

energisch (G.) Same as ÉNERGIQUE.

énervant, en s' (F.) Becoming nervous or irritable, fidgeting.

enfatico (It.) Exaggerated, pompous, with undue emphasis. Also, **con enfasi.**

englisches Horn (G.) English horn.

énigmatique (F.) Mysterious.

enjoué (F.) Cheerful, jovial. Also, **avec enjouement.**

enlevez (F.) Remove, e.g., *enlevez pédal,* remove pedal, *enlevez les sourdines,* remove the mutes.

ensemble (F.) (1) Group of performers. (2) Together.

entêtement, avec (F.) Stubbornly, persistently.

enthousiasme, avec (F.) With enthusiasm, vigorously.

enthusiastisch (G.) Enthusiastic.

entrain, avec (F.) Briskly, with animation, spirited.

entrainant (F.) Eloquently, winningly, captivating.

entreé (F.) Entrance.

entrückt (G.) Withdrawn, removed, distant.

entschieden (G.) Determined, decided.

entschlossen (G.) Same as ENTSCHIEDEN.

entusiasmandosi (It.) Enthusiastic, enraptured. Also,

con entusiasmo.

entusiasmo, con (Sp.) Vigorously, enthusiastically.

Entzücken (G.) Delight. Also, **entzückt,** delighted.

enveloppé (F.) Muffled.

éperdu (F.) Bewildered, distraught.

épouvante surgit, l' (F.) With rising terror.

épuisement (F.) Drained, exhausted.

equabile (It.) Evenly, smoothly. Also, **equabilmente.**

equilibrado (Sp.) Balanced.

ergänzend (G.) Supplementing, supporting.

ergeben (G.) (1) To yield. (2) Devoted to, faithful.

ergebungsvoll (G.) Submissive, resigned. Also, **mit Ergebung.**

ergriffen (G.) Deeply moved. Also, **mit Ergriffenheit,** (rarely) **ergreifen.**

erhaben (G.) Lofty, exalted, grand.

erheblich (G.) Considerably, a great deal.

erhoben (G.) Raised, louder, e.g., *mit erhobener Stimme*, in a louder voice.

erlöschend (G.) Fading away.

ermattend (G.) Weakening, becoming softer.

ermunternd (G.) Enlivened, animated.

ernst (G.) Serious, earnest. Also, ernsthaft.

ernstlich (G.) Fervent, ardent, with genuine feeling.

eroiccomico (It.) Mock-heroic.

eroico (It.) Heroic, dramatic, melodramatic.

erompente (It.) Bursting forth.

erregt (G.) Excited, agitated, e.g., *mit erregter Stimme*, in an excited tone. Also, mit Erregung.

erreichten Tempo, im (G.) Present tempo.

erschöpft (G.) Exhausted.

erschrocken (G.) Startled, frightened.

Erschütterung, mit (G.) Shaken, trembling, with strong feeling.

erst (G.) First, original, e.g.,

erstes Tempo, original tempo.

ersterbend (G.) Fading away.

eruttivo (It.) Eruptive, bursting out.

erzählend (G.) Telling, narrative; sometimes, recitative.

Erzähler (G.) In organs, a foundation stop.

Es (G.) E-flat.

esagerando (It.) Exaggerating, excessive. Also, esagerato.

esaltatissimo (It.) Very excited, elated, with great fervor. Also, con esaltazione, esaltato.

esatto (It.) Precise, exact, e.g., *esatto il ritmo*, in precise rhythm, *in tempo esatto*, in exact tempo. Also, esattamente.

Eses (G.) E-double-flat.

esitando (It.) Hesitant, wavering. Also, con esitazione, esitante.

esp. (It.) Short for ESPRESSIVO.

espansivo (It.) Exuberant, broad. Also, con espansione.

espirando (It.) (1) Exhaling, (2) Fading away.

espiritu, con (Sp.) With spirit, boldly.

espressivo (It.) With expression, with feeling. Also, **esp., espr., express., con espressione.**

esquerda (Port.) Left (hand).

estando (It.) Becoming broader, and, usually, louder.

estatico (It.) Rapturous, overwhelmed with joy.

estilo (Sp.) Style.

estinguendosi (It.) Dying away.

estinto (It.) Very softly, barely audible.

estompé (F.) Toned down, muffled.

estremamente (It.) Very, exceedingly. Also, **estremo.**

estribillo (Sp.) Refrain.

esuberante (It.) Lively and loud.

esultante (It.) Rejoicing.

et (F.) And.

éteignant, en s' (F.) Dying away.

éteint (F.) Very soft.

étincelant (F.) Sparkling, brilliant.

étonnement, avec (F.) With astonishment.

étouffé (F.) (1) Damped, i.e., damp sound immediately (in harps, cymbals, etc.). (2) Stifled, choked, muted.

étrange (F.) Strange, odd. Also, **étrangeté**, strangeness.

etwas (G.) Somewhat.

évanouissant, s' (F.) Becoming faint.

évaporant, en (F.) Disappearing.

éveillé (F.) Brisk, animated.

eventuell (G.) Perhaps, possibly.

evidente (It.) In evidence, present, audible, e.g., *pianissimo ma evidente*, very soft but audible.

evvivando (It.) Becoming loud, cheering.

ex- (It.) For Italian words, see under *es-*, e.g., for *extatico*, see ESTATICO.

exactamente (Sp.) Strictly.

exagération (F.) Exaggeration.

exaltación, con (Sp.) Exuberant, elevated.

excessivement (F.) Extremely.

expresivo (Sp.) Same as ESPRESSIVO. Also, **con expresión.**

expressif (F.) Same as ESPRESSIVO.

extasis, con (Sp.) Rapturous.

extatique (F.) Rapturous.

F

f (It.) Short for FORTE.

fa (F., It., Sp.) The note or key of F, e.g., (It.), *corni in fa,* F horns.

facile (F., It.) Free, easy, flowing. Also, (F.) **facilement, avec facilité.**

façon, sans (F.) Simply, unaffected.

fagot (Sp.) Bassoon.

Fagott (G.) Bassoon.

fagotto (It.) (1) Bassoon. (2) In organs, an important reed stop.

falsete (Sp.) Falsetto.

falsettirend (G.) In falsetto. Also, **Falsett.**

falsetto (It.) High-pitched and light in quality, like the falsetto voice.

fanatisch (G.) Fanatical, wild.

fanfara (It.) Fanfare.

fantaisie, avec (F.) Freely, capriciously, whimsically. Also, **fantaisiste.**

fantasia, con (It., Sp.) Freely, with imagination.

Fantasieenmässig (G.) See PHANTASIEENMÄSSIG.

fantastico (It.) Fanciful, irregular.

Färbung (G.) Color, tone, e.g., *mit trüber Färbung,* with a dull tone.

farouche (F.) Wild, fierce.

farruco (Sp.) Bold, daring, impudent.

Fassung (G.) Version, e.g., *erste Fassung,* first version.

fastidio, con (It.) With annoyance.

fastoso (It.) Pompous, ostentatious.

fausse, faux (F.) False, deceptive.

fausset, en (F.) Head voice, falsetto.

febbrile (It.) Feverish, very excited.

feierlich (G.) Solemn, stately.

Feldflöte (G) In organs, same as WALDFLÖTE.

felice (It.) Happy, glad, exultant.

feltro (It.) Muffled.

fermamente (It.) Steadily, unwaveringly. Also, **fermo, con fermezza.**

fermata (It.) A pause or hold (longer-held note or rest), usually indicated by ⌒ .

Fermate (G.) Same as FERMATA.

fermé (F.) Closed. Also, **fermez, fermer.**

fermeté, avec (F.) Firmly, resolutely.

fern (G.) Faraway, distant. Also, **wie aus der Ferne**, as though from a distance.

feroce (It.) Fierce, harsh, wild.

ferre da calza, con (It.) With knitting needles.

fervent (F.) Enthusiastic, devoted.

fervido (It.) Ardent, impassioned.

fervore, con (It.) With vehemence, ardently.

Fes (G.) F-flat.

fest (G.) Solid, firm, thorough, e.g., *fest betont*, firmly accented.

festivamente (It.) Joyfully, cheerfully. Also, **festivo.**

festlich (G.) Festive, solemn.

festoso (It.) Merry, gay.

feu, avec (F.) With fire, passionately.

feurig (G.) Fiery, spirited. Also, **mit Feuer.**

ff (It.) Short for FORTISSIMO. Also, **fff.**

fiacco (It.) Weak, feeble.

fiato (It.) Breath, e.g., *in un sol fiato*, in a single breath, *stromenti di fiato*, wind instruments.

fieberhaft (G.) Excited, restless.

fier, fière (F.) Haughty, bold.

fieramente (It.) Vehemently, boldly. Also, **fiero, con fierezza.**

fièvreux (F.) Feverish, restless, excited.

fila la voce (It.) In vocal music, prolong a note while first swelling and then diminishing in volume.

filer la voix (F.) Same as FILA LA VOCE.

filo di voce (It.) Very faint, barely audible (voice).

Filz (G.) Felt (i.e., felt-covered beater).

fin (F., Sp.) End.

fine (It.) End.

finement (F.) Artfully, with skill.

finezza, con (It.) With refinement, elegant.

Fingersatz (G.) Fingering.

fino (It.) Until, up to. Also, **fin'**, e.g., *fin' al segno*, up to the sign.

finster (G.) Dark, somber, sad.

finzione, senza (It.) Open, frank.

fior di labbra, a (It.) See LABBRA, A FIOR DI.

Fis (G.) F-sharp.

fisarmonica (It.) Accordion.

Fisis (G.) F-double-sharp.

fisso (It.) Steady, firm.

Fistelstimme (G.) Falsetto.

fitto (It.) Firmly.

fl. (F., It.) Short for flute(s).

Flachflöte (G.) In organs, an open flute stop.

flageolet (F.) (1) An old wind instrument, a type of flute. (2) In organs, an open flute stop. (3) Harmonics.

flageolet harmonique (F.) In organs, an open flute stop.

Flageolette (G.) Harmonics. Also, **Flag.**

Flatterzunge (G.) Flutter tonguing.

flauta (Sp.) Flute.

flautada (It.) In organs, a loud, low-pitched foundation stop.

flautando (It.) (1) Flutelike, that is, a light pure tone with few overtones. (2) In stringed instruments (harp, violin, etc.), producing harmonics. (3) In bowing, a tone produced by bowing gently but fast over the fingerboard. Also, **flautato.**

flautín (Sp.) Piccolo.

flautino (It.) (1) Piccolo. (2) Any small flute or recorder. (3) In organs, an open flute stop.

flauto (It.) Flute.

flauto amabile (It.) In organs, same as AMOROSA.

flauto d'amore (It.) In organs, same as FLÛTE D'AMOUR.

flauto dolce (It.) In organs, a very soft open flute stop. Also, **dolce flute, flûte douce.**

flauto mirabilis (It. + L.) In organs, a loud open flute stop with brilliant tone.

flautone (It.) Bass flute.

flauto traverso (It.) (1) Older name for the orchestral flute. (2) In organs, an important open flute stop designed to imitate the tone of the orchestral flute.

flebile (It.) Plaintive, weak, mournful.

flehend (G.) Beseeching, imploring.

flessibile (It.) Agile, flexible.

flicorno (It.) Flugelhorn.

fliessend (G.) Flowing, smooth.

flimmernd (G.) Flickering, wavering.

Flöte (G.) Flute.

Flötenbass (G.) In organs, an open flute stop usually controlled by the pedals. Also, **bass flute, flûte bass.**

flott (G.) Briskly, without hesitation.

flottant (F.) Flowing, drifting, irresolute.

flou, floue (F.) Hazy, blurred, indistinct.

fl. picc. (It.) Short for piccolo(s).

flüchtig (G.) Fleeting, skimming over the notes.

fluente (It.) Flowing, pulsating, wave-like.

Flügelhorn (G.) (1) Flugelhorn. (2) In organs, a solo reed stop designed to imitate the tone of the flugelhorn.

fluide (F.) Flowing, smooth.

fluido (It.) Same as FLUIDE.

flüssig (G.) Same as FLUIDE. Also, **mit Fluss.**

flüsternd (G.) Whispering, rustling.

flûte (F.) Flute.

flûte à bec (F.) (1) Recorder. (2) In organs, a soft stop designed to imitate the tone of the recorder.

flûte céleste (F.) In organs, a fairly soft undulating flute stop.

flûte d'amour (F.) In organs, a soft flute stop. Also, **flauto d'amore.**

flûte douce (F.) In organs, same as FLAUTO DOLCE.

flutend (G.) Surging, flowing.

flûte ouverte (F.) In organs, an important open flute stop.

flûte triangulaire (F.) In organs, an open flute stop whose pipes are triangular in cross-section.

focosamente (It.) Fiery, ardent, impetuous.

fois (F.) Time(s), e.g., *deux fois*, two times (twice).

folgen (G.) Follow, accompany. Also, **folgend.**

fond (F.) Foundation stop.

fond de train, à (F.) At full speed, very fast.

fond doux (F.) A soft foundation stop.

fondu (F.) Becoming softer, dying away.

force, avec (F.) Vigorously, boldly.

forse (It.) Perhaps.

fort (It.) (1) Loud. (2) Very, e.g., *fort peu*, very little. (3) (G.) Off (organ stops).

forte (It.) Loud. Also, *f.*

fortepiano (It.) Loud, then soft. Also, *fp.*

fortissimo (It.) Very loud. Also, *ff, fff.*

fortsetzend (G.) Continuing, resuming.

fortwährend (G.) Constant, continuous, incessant.

forza, con (It.) Powerful, forceful, loud.

forzando (It.) A sharp accent. Also, **forzato,** *fz.*

forzare (It.) To force, to strain, e.g., *forzare la voce*, forcing the voice.

foudroyant (F.) Thundering.

fouetté (F.) Lifting the bow off the string and then whipping it down onto the string.

fougueux (F.) Fierce, fiery, spirited.

fourniture (F.) In organs, one of the most important mixture stops.

fp (It.) Short for FORTEPIANO.

fragile (F., It.) Weak, soft.

frais, fraîche (F.) Fresh, brisk.

franchement (F.) Openly, simply, sincerely. Also, **avec franchise.**

frapper (F.) To strike, to pound.

frase (It.) Musical phrase.

fraseggio (It.) Phrasing, articulation.

freddo (It.) Cold, without emotion.

fregando (It.) Rubbing, brushing against, applying friction to.

frei (G.) Free, especially in free tempo.

frei deklamieren (G.) Free recitative.

fremente (It.) (1) Raging, roaring. (2) Quivering, trembling.

frémissant (F.) Trembling.

fremito, come un (It.) (1) Like a roar. (2) Like a tremor.

frenare (It.) To restrain, to hold back.

frenetico (It.) Wild, furious, frenzied.

frénétique (F.) Wild, raving.

freschezza, con (It.) In a fresh, pure style.

frettoloso (It.) Hasty, hurried. Also, **frettoso.**

freudig (G.) Happy, joyful.

freudiger Bewegung, mit (G.) With joyful animation. Also, **mit freudiger Regung.**

freundlich (G.) Friendly, affable.

Frieden, mit (G.) Peacefully, quietly. Also, **friedlich, mit Friedlichkeit.**

frisch (G.) (1) Brisk, gay. Also, **mit Frische.** (2) Fresh, new.

frissonant (F.) Fluttering, trembling.

frivol (G.) Impudent, flippant. Also, **mit Frivolität.**

frivolo (It.) Trifling, frivolous.

froh (G.) Happy.

fröhlich (G.) Joyful.

frohlockend (G.) Jubilant, triumphant.

fromm (G.) Devout, pious.

Frosch, am (G.) At the frog end of the bow.

früher (G.) Earlier, before, e.g., *wie früher*, as before, *früheres Tempo*, (the) previous tempo.

frullato (It.) (1) Hummed, buzzing. (2) Fluttery, agitated.

fruscio (It.) Rustle, murmur. Also, **frusciante.**

fuerte (Sp.) Loud.

fuerza, con (Sp.) Forcefully, loudly.

fugara (It.) In organs, a fairly loud string stop.

fuggevole (It.) Fleeting, rapid. Also, **fuggitivo.**

führend (G.) Leading, uppermost.

fulgurant (F.) Lightning flashes.

funèbre (F.) Funereal, e.g., *marche funèbre*, funeral march.

fúnebre (Sp.) Gloomy, sad.

funereo (It.) Sad, mournful. Also, **funebre.**

fuoco, con (It.) With fire, passionately, excited.

fuori, di (It.) From outside (from backstage).

furiant (Czech.) Lively dance in rapid 3/4 tempo, with syncopated rhythms.

furioso (It.) Wild, passionate. Also, **con furia.**

furtif, futive (F.) Stealthy. Also, **furtivement.**

fusa (Sp.) Thirty-second note.

fuso (It.) Joined together, bound.

fuyant (F.) Fleeing, fleeting, fading away.

fz (It.) Short for FORZANDO.

G

gagliardo (It.) Robust, powerful, vigorous.

gai, gaie (F.) Merry, cheerful. Also, **gaiement, gaîment, avec gaîté (gaieté).**

gaillard (F.) Happy, gay, sprightly.

gaio (It.) Gay, joyful. Also, **con gaiezza.**

gallardía, con (Sp.) Nobly, elegantly.

galoppo, al (It.) At a gallop, very fast.

gamba (It.) (1) Short for viola da gamba, the old bass viol. (2)) In organs, an important string stop, with a brilliant, moderately loud tone. Also, (F.) **gambe.**

ganz (G.) Quite, wholly, very, e.g., *ganz langsam*, very slow.

ganze (G.) Whole note (*ganze Note*) or whole rest (*ganze Pause*).

garbato (It.) Graceful, elegant. Also, (It., Sp.) **con garbo.**

gauche (F.) Left (hand).

gavotta (It.) Gavotte.

gebunden (G.) Tied, LEGATO.

Gedackt (G.) In organs, an important stopped flute pipe. Also, **Gedeckt.**

gedämpft (G.) Muted, muffled.

Gedeckt (G.) Same as GEDACKT.

Gedecktpommer (G.) In organs, a stopped flute stop. Also, **Pommer.**

gedehnt (G.) Dragging, slow.

gedrängt (G.) Compact, compressed.

Gefallen, nach (G.) As one wishes.

gefasst (G.) Calm, tranquil, resigned.

gefühlvoll (G.) With feeling, tenderly. Also, **mit Gefühl.**

gehalten (G.) Held, sustained.

geheimnisvoll (G.) Mysterious.

gehend (G.) Moving at a moderate tempo, same as ANDANTE. Also, **gehender.**

gehetzt (G.) Driven.

Geige (G.) Violin.

Geigenbass (G.) In organs, a low-pitched foundation stop of diapason tone.

gekichert (G.) Giggled, tittered.

gekoppelt (G.) Coupled.

gelassen (G.) Quiet, calm, unhurried.

geläufig (G.) Flowing, smooth.

gélido (Sp.) Icy, frigid.

gelöster (G.) Looser, freer.

gemach (G.) Softly and gently, gradually.

gemächlich (G.) Comfortable, leisurely.

gemässigt (G.) Moderate tempo.

gemendo (It.) Lamenting.

gemessen (G.) At a regular pace, in steady rhythm.

gemischt (G.) Mixed, e.g., *gemischte Stimmen*, mixed voices.

Gemshorn (G.) In organs, an important foundation stop.

gemütlich (G.) Comfortable, leisurely.

gentilmente (It.) Gently, with refinement.

gentiment (F.) Prettily, daintily.

gepresst (G.) (1) Crowded, overfull. (2) In vocal music, in a choked voice. (3) Depressed, dejected.

gering, geringer, geringes (G.) Little, smaller.

gerissen (G.) (1) Dragged, pulled along. (2) Cunning, sly.

gerührt (G.) To feel moved or deeply touched.

Ges (G.) G-flat.

gesammelt (G.) Gathered together.

Gesang (G.) Singing, voice, vocal part.

gesanglich (G.) Vocal.

gesangvoll (G.) Songlike, lyrical. Also, **gesangartig, gesangreich.**

gesättigt (G.) Satisfied, full, e.g., *mit gesättigtem Ton*, with a full tone.

geschäftig (G.) Bustling, stirring.

geschlagen (G.) Struck, e.g., *mit dem Bogen geschlagen*, hitting the bow (against the strings).

geschleift (G.) Slurred, bound, LEGATO.

geschlossen (G.) Closed.

geschmeidig (G.) Flexible, agile, glib, e.g., *mit geschmeidiger Bewegung*, with flexible movement, with agility.

geschwind (G.) Quick, nimble.

Geses (G.) G-double-flat.

gespannt (G.) (1) Restless, expectant, tense. (2) Drawn out.

gespenstig (G.) Ghostly. Also, **gespentisch.**

gesperrt (G.) Spaced out, spread.

gesprochen (G.) Spoken.

gesteigert (G.) Increased, intensified, louder.

gestopft (G.) Stopped (in horns).

gestossen (G.) Abrupt, disconnected, STACCATO.

gestrafft (G.) Tight, tense, concise.

gestrichen (G.) (1) Bowed. (2) Passing over softly and smoothly, LEGATO. (3) In notation, describing notes above or below the staff, which require ledger lines.

gesummt (G.) Hummed.

gesungen (G.) Sung.

geteilt (G.) Same as DIVISI; *nicht geteilt*, not divisi (i.e., UNISONO).

getragen (G.) Sustained and slow, same as SOSTENUTO.

gettato (It.) Same as JETÉ. Also, **gettate.**

gewichtig (G.) Weighty, pompous.

gewissen (G.) (1) Particular, certain, e.g., *mit einem gewissen Schwung*, with a certain lilt. (2) Conscience, e.g., *ein gutes Gewissen*, a clear conscience.

gewöhnlich (G.) (1) Ordinary, as usual, simple. (2) Normal position of bow.

geworfen (G.) Same as SPICCATO.

gezogen (G.) Drawn out, sustained.

giocondamente (It.) Joyfully, happily. Also, **giocondo.**

giocoso (It.) Jocose, humorous. Also, **giocando, con gioco.**

gioioso (It.) Joyous, cheerful. Also, **con gioia.**

Gis (G.) G-sharp.

Gisis (G.) G-double-sharp.

gitana, alla (It.) In gypsy style.

Gitarre (G.) Guitar.

giubilando (It.) Rejoicing, exultant. Also, **giubilante, giubiloso, con giubilo.**

giudaïco, in modo (It.) In the Jewish manner (like Jewish chant).

giulivo (It.) Merry, festive, joyful.

giuocando (It.) Same as GIOCOSO.

giusto (It.) Exact, right, appropriate, e.g., *tempo giusto*, appropriate tempo (or strict tempo).

glänzend (G.) Brilliant, splendid. Also, **glanzvoll.**

glas, comme un (F.) Like a death knell.

glashart (G.) Clear, crystalline, brilliant.

gleich (G.) (1) The same. Also, **gleiches, gleicher.** (2) Immediately, at once.

gleichförmig (G.) Equal, uniform, even.

gleichgültig (G.) Careless, casual, indifferent.

gleichmässig (G.) Even, regular.

gleitend (G.) Gliding, smooth.

gli (It.) The.

glissando (pseud. It.) A glide from one note to the next. Also, **gliss.**

glissez (F.) Slide (over the notes), a GLISSANDO.

glitzernd (G.) Sparkling.

Glocke (G.) Bell.

Glockenspiel (G.) In organs, same as CARILLON (2).

glorioso (It.) Glorious, splendid.

glühend (G.) Glowing, ablaze, fervent.

goffaggine, con una (It.) Awkwardly, clumsily. Also, **goffamente.**

Gong (G.) Gong.

gosier, dans le (F.) In the throat.

goutte, une (F.) A drop, like a raindrop.

gracia, con (Sp.) Graceful. Also, **gracioso, graciosamente.**

gracieux, gracieuse (F.) Graceful, elegant. Also, **gracieusement, avec grâce.**

gracile (It.) Delicate, graceful. Also, **gracilmente.**

gracioso (Sp.) (1) Graceful, refined. (2) Witty, humorous. (3) Jester, clown.

gradatamente (It.) Gradually, step by step.

gradazione, con (It.) By degrees, subtly shading.

gradevole (It.) Pleasant, pleasing. Also, **gradevolmente.**

grado a grado (It.) By degrees. Also, **per gradi.**

grado a grado la corda (It.) Scale step by scale step on the string.

graduatamente (It.) Gradually.

gran cassa (It.) Bass drum. Also, **gran tamburo, gr. cassa, g. cassa.**

grand bourdon (F.) In organs, a special mixture stop made up of several ranks of stopped flute pipes.

grand-choeur (F.) Full organ.

grand détaché (F.) In bowing, alternate up- and down-bows, but with long strokes. (See also DÉTACHÉ.)

grande (It.) Broadly.

grandendo (It.) Becoming broader.

grandezza, con (It.) With grandeur, stately. Also (It., Sp.) **grandioso.**

grand-orgue (F.) Great organ. Also, **G^d-o.**

grave (F., It.) (1) Flat, low-pitched. (2) Solemn, serious, slow. Also (F.) **gravement, avec gravité,** (It.) **gravemente, con gravità.**

gravissima (It.) In organs, a very low-pitched bass stop on the pedals. Also, **acoustic bass, resultant, vox gravissima.**

gravità, con (It.) Dignified, serious.

gravitätisch (G.) Grave, solemn.

grazia, con (It.) With grace, prettily.

graziös (G.) Graceful.

grazioso (It.) Graceful and easy, ANDANTE.

grell (G.) Shrill, strident.

grelots (F.) Sleighbells.

Gr. Fl. (F., G.) Short for flute (as opposed to piccolo).

grida (It.) Proclamation.

gridando (It.) Shouting. Also, **gridato.**

Griffbrett, am (G.) On the fingerboard. Also, **auf dem Griffbrett.**

grimmig (G.) Fierce, raging, vehement, intense.

grive musicienne (F.) Song thrush.

grollend (G.) Angry, sullen.

gros, grosse (F.) Rough, loud, massive.

gross, grosse, grosser (G.) Large.

grosse caisse (F.) Bass drum.

Grosse Trommel (G.) Bass drum.

Grossflöte (G.) In organs, an 8-foot open flute stop on both manuals and pedals.

grossièrement (F.) Roughly.

grossissant la voix, en (F.) Swelling, becoming louder and louder.

grossolano (It.) Rough, coarse, crude.

grotesk (G.) Fantastic, grotesque.

grottescamente (It.) Grotesquely, fancifully. Also, **grottesco.**

Grundeinheit (G.) Basic unit, basic meter.

Grundtempo (G.) Basic tempo.

gruppo (It.) A turn. Also, **gruppetto.**

guajira (Sp.) (1) A type of Cuban popular song. (2) Rustic, boorish.

guerra, alla (It.) In a martial style.

guilleret (F.) Lively, brisk.

guitare (F.) Guitar.

guitarra (Sp.) Guitar.

gusto, con (It.) With style, with zest.

gut (G.) Good, e.g., *gut gelaunt*, in good humor. (2) Well, thoroughly, e.g., *gut rhythmisiert*, thoroughly rhythmic.

H

H (G.) The note B.

habanera (Sp.) A Cuban dance with distinctive rhythm.

habgierig (G). Greedy, grasping.

haché (F.) Choppy, abrupt, irregular

halb (G.) Half, e.g., *halb gesungen*, half sung.

Halbe (G.) Half note (*Halbe Note*) or half rest (*Halbe Pause*).

Halbton (G.) Half tone, semitone.

haletant (F.) Panting, grasping.

Hälfte (G.) Half, e.g., *die erste Hälfte*, the first half.

Haltung (G.) Pause, fermata.

Harfe (G.) Harp.

Harfenprinzipal (G.) In organs, a soft diapason stop.

harmonia aetheria (L.) In organs, a soft manual mixture stop.

harmonie (F., G. cap.) (1) Harmony, chords. (2) (G.) Older name for wind band, wind section.

harmonieux (F.) Melodious.

Harmonika (G.) In organs, an 8-foot manual open flute stop. Also, harmonica.

harpe (F.) Harp.

hart (G.) Hard, firm, solid.

Hartfilz (G.) A hard felt beater (for drums).

hasta (Sp.) Up to, until, e.g., *hasta la extinción del sonido,* until the sound ceases.

hastig (G.) (1) With haste, hurrying. Also, hastend. (2) Abrubtly, suddenly.

hâte, sans (F.) Without haste, easily, deliberately. Also, ne hâtez pas.

Hauch, wie ein (G.) Like a breath, very lightly.

Hauptstimme (G.) (1) Prinicpal voice or part. (2) Melody.

Hauptzeitmass (G.) Main tempo.

hautbois (F.) (1) Oboe. (2) In organs, an 8-foot manual reed stop designed to sound like the orchestral oboe.

hautbois d'amour (F.) Same as OBOE D'AMORE.

heftig (G.) (1) Violent, strong. (2) Very, e.g., *heftig bewegt,* very lively.

heilig (G.) Holy, sacred.

heimlich (G.) Mysterious, stealthily.

heiser (G.) Hoarse, e.g., *mit heiserer Stimme,* with a hoarse voice.

heiter (G.) Cheerful, gay.

heldenhaft (G.) Heroically, in a stalwart manner.

hell (G.) Clear, ringing.

Hellflöte (G.) In organs, an open flute stop with a loud, bright tone.

hemidemisemiquaver (Brit.) Sixty-fourth note.

herantrippelnd (G.) Tripping along.

herausheben (G.) Emphasize, set off (from the background).

héroïque (F.) Noble, grand.

herrisch (G.) Overbearing, haughty.

Herunterstrich (G.) Down-bow.

hervor (G.) Forward, bring out, emphasize. Also, **hervorheben.**

hervorbrechend (G.) Bursting out.

hervorgehoben (G.) Emphasized, accented.

hervortretend (G.) Standing out, emphasized.

herzlich (G.) Hearty, warm, sincere.

hésitant (F.) Wavering, hanging back.

heurté (F.) Abrupt, harsh, jerky.

Hinaufstrich (G.) Up-bow. Also, **Hinstrich.**

Hingebung, mit (G.) Enthusiastically, faithfully. Also, **hingebend.**

hingeworfen (G.) Quick, flighty.

hinhaltend (G.) Holding back, delaying.

hinsterbend (G.) Fading away.

hinströmend (G.) Flowing.

hintersinnig (G.) Melancholy, sad.

His (G.) B-sharp.

hoch (G.) High, upward, e.g., *Stürzen hoch,* bells up.

Höhepunkt (G.) Climax.

hohl (G.) Hollow, dull, muffled.

Hohlflöte (G.) In organs, an open flute stop. Also, **Hohlpfeife.**

höhnisch (G.) Derisive, mocking, scornful. Also, **höhnend.**

Holzrankett (G.) In organs, a rankett stop with wooden (instead of metal) resonators.

Holzregal (G.) In organs, a wooden reed stop.

hörbar (G.) Audible.

Horn (G.) Usually, French horn. Sometimes, saxhorn. Also, **Hörner** (pl.).

huitième de soupir (F.) Thirty-second rest.

humeur, avec (F.) With humor, fanciful.

Humor, mit (G) With humor, facetiously. Also, **humorvoll.**

humoristico (Sp.) Jovial, amiable.

hüpfend (G.) Skipping, hopping.

hurtig (G.) Rapid, agile.

huschend (G.) Scurrying, gliding by.

hymnenartig (G.) Hymnlike. Also, **hymnisch.**

I

i (It.) The.

Iº (It.) Short for primo (see PRIMA).

idyllisch (G.) Idyllic, pastoral.

ieratico (It.) Solemn, stylized.

igual (Sp.) Even, uniform.

il (It.) The.

im (G.) In the.

imitando (It.) Imitating, echoing.

immer (G.) Always, constantly, e.g., *immer gleiches Zeitmass*, always in the same tempo.

immobile (It.) Motionless.

impavido (It.) Fearless, undaunted.

imperceptible (Sp.) Very soft, scarcely audible.

impérieux (F.) Commanding, haughty.

imperioso (It., Sp.) Stately, dignified, commanding.

impeto, con (It.) With violence, rushing in.

impétueux (F.) Impetuous, vehement, headlong. Also, **impétueusement.**

impetuoso (It.) Violent, impetuous.

implacable (F.) Unyielding, unrelenting, constant, e.g., *vitesse implacable*, constantly very fast.

implorant (F.) Beseeching.

improvisant, en (F.) Improvising.

improvisation, comme une (F.) As though improvised.

improvvisando (It.) Improvising, freely, ad lib. Also, **improvvisamente.**

inbrünstig (G.) Ardent, passionate.

incalzando (It.) Pressing on, hurrying.

incamminando (It.) Setting forth, initiating.

incantando (It.) Enchanting, delighting.

incisif (F.) Sharp, precise.

incisivo (It.) Incisive, clear-cut, sharply delineated. Also, **inciso.**

incolore (F., It.) Steady, without color or emphasis.

incubo, come in (It.) As in a nightmare.

indécis (F.) Hesitant, wavering.

indifférent (F.) Without emotion.

indifferente (It.) Apathetic.

indistinto (It.) Blurred, vague, faint.

indolemment (F.) Lazily.

indolente (It.) Listless, apathetic.

in due (It.) See DUE, IN.

indugiando (It.) Delaying, retarding.

inflessione (It.) (1) Inflection, e.g., *inflessione di voce,* vocal inflection, *senza inflessioni,* without inflections. (2) Flexibility, e.g., *inflessione di tempo,*

a flexible tempo, not too strict.

inflexible (F.) Firm, decisive, unwavering.

infuorandosi (It.) Becoming enraged. Also, **infuriando.**

ingenuità, con (It.) Innocently, simply, sincerely.

ingénuo (Sp.) Open, candid, artless. Also, (Port.) **ingênuo,** (Sp.) **ingenuamente.**

iniziale (It.) Original, e.g., *tempo iniziale,* original tempo. Also, **inizio** *(tempo d'inizio).*

inner, innere, inneres (G.) Inner, interior, e.g., *innere Stimme,* inner voice-part.

innig (G.) Heartfelt, fervent. Also, **inniglich, mit Innigkeit.**

innocemment (F.) Simple, artless.

innodia, come una (It.) Hymnlike.

inocente (Sp.) Simple, plain.

inquiet (F.) Uneasy, agitated.

inquieto (It.) Restless, uneasy.

insensibilmente (It.) Very slightly, scarcely at all.

inserirsi (It.) Inserted, interpolated.

insidioso (It.) Treacherously, insidiously, insinuated.

insinuante (It.) Suggested.

insistenza, con (It.) Obstinate, persistent. Also, **insistendo.**

inspirant, en (F.) Inhaling.

intensiv (G.) Intense, ardent, vehement.

intensificando (It.) Intensifying, becoming louder.

intenso (It.) Intense, violent. Also, **intensito, intensamente, con intensità.**

intenzione, con (It.) Purposeful, deliberate. Also, **intenzionato.**

intimement (F.) Intimately, confidentially, quietly.

intimo (It., Sp.) Intimately, familiar.

intrepido (It.) Fearless, undaunted, bold.

invocando (It.) Calling upon.

ipnoticamente (It.) Hypnotically.

irato (It.) Furious, enraged.

irisé (F.) Iridescent, shimmering.

ironico (It.) Ironical.

ironique (F.) Mocking.

irrationnel (F.) Unequal.

irréel (F.) Imaginary, fanciful, otherworldly. Also, **irréelment.**

irrequieto (It.) Restless, uneasy.

irresoluto (It.) Uncertain, tentative.

irritant, en s' (F.) Becoming angry.

irritato (It.) Provoked, annoyed.

islancio, con (It.) With dash, with verve.

isoritmico (It.) Isorhythmic, i.e., repeating a fixed rhythmic pattern.

istesso tempo, l' (It.) At the same tempo. Also, **lo stesso tempo.**

izquierdo (Sp.) Left (hand).

J

j For Italian words, see under *gi-*, e.g., for *jubilo*, see GIUBILO.

jauchzend (G.) Shouting with joy, exultant, cheering.

jede, jeder, jedes (G.) Every, any.

jedesmal (G.) Every time, always.

jedoch (G.) Yet, still, nevertheless.

jeté (F.) Throwing the bow against the string, making contact in its upper third, so that it will rebound several times on the down-bow.

jeu (F.) Organ stop.

jeu de clochette (F.) In organs, a manual mixture stop.

jeux doux (F.) Soft organ stops.

jeux forts (F.) Loud organ stops.

jocoso (Sp.) Humorous.

joyeux (F.) Happy, lighthearted. Also, **joyeusement.**

Jubalflöte (G.) In organs, same as SERAPHONFLÖTE.

jubelnd (G.) Rejoicing, exulting. Also, **jubilierend.**

juego de timbres (Sp.) Glockenspiel. Also, **órgano de campanas.**

jünglingshaften (G.) Youthful.

juntos (Sp.) Together.

jusqu'à (F.) Up to, e.g., *jusqu'à la fin,* up to the end.

K

Kadenz (G.) (1) Cadence. (2) Cadenza.

kadenzartig (G.) Like a cadenza.

kapriziös (G.) Willful, capricious, whimsical.

karikiert (G.) Caricatured.

kaum (G.) Scarcely, hardly, e.g., *kaum betont,* scarcely accented, *kaum hörbar,* scarcely audible.

keck (G.) Bold, impudent.

keifend (G.) Scolding, jangling, yelping.

kein, keine, keiner (G.) No, none, e.g., *keine Betonung,* no accent.

klagend (G.) Lamenting, plaintive. Also, **kläglich.**

Klang (G.) Sound.

klangvoll (G.) Ringing, resounding.

Klappe (G.) Key or valve (in wind instruments).

klar (G.) Clear, distinct.

Klarinette (G.) Clarinet.

Klavier (G.) Piano.

Klavierauszug (G.) Arrangement for piano.

kleine Mixture (G.) In organs, a soft manual mixture stop.

Kleinerzähler (G.) In organs, a 4-foot manual foundation stop.

Kleinflöte (G.) In organs, a 4-foot manual flute stop.

Kleinprinzipal (G.) In organs, 4-foot foundation stop on the manuals.

klingen lassen (G.) Let sound.

klingt (G.) Rings, sounds.

Knopfregal (G.) In organs, a reed stop of the regal group.

kokett (G.) Flirtatious.

Kontrabass (G.) Double bass, contrabass.

Kontrafagott (G.) Contrabassoon.

Koppel (G.) Coupler.

Koppelflöte (G.) In organs, an open flute stop.

Kornett (G.) Cornet.

kosend (G.) Caressingly, fondly.

Kraft, mit (G.) Vigorously, forcefully. Also, **kräftig, kraftvoll.**

kreischend (G.) Strident, shrill.

Krummhorn (G.) (1) Crumhorn (obsolete woodwind). (2) In organs, an 8-foot solo reed stop on the manuals. Also, (F., It.) **cromorne.**

kurz, kurze, kurzer (G.) Short, brief, e.g., *kurzer Halt*, short pause.

L

l' (F.) The.

la (1) (F., It., Sp.) The. (2) The note and key of A, e.g. (It.), *clarinetto in la*, A clarinet.

labbra (It.) Lip.

labbra, a fior di (It.) At the front of the mouth, i.e., very lightly and softly sung or spoken.

lacerante (It.) Tearing, rending.

lâchez (F.) Release.

lacrimoso (It.) Mournful, Tearful. Also, lagrimoso.

Lage (G.) Position (in playing violins, etc.).

lagnoso (It.) Lamenting, miserable.

lagrimoso (Sp.) Same as LACRIMOSO.

laissez (F.) (1) Depart, leave, leave alone. (2) Let, e.g., *laissez vibrer*, let sound (or release damper).

lamento, con (It.) Mournful, plaintive. Also, lamentevole, lamentoso.

lancer (F.) To launch, to begin, e.g., *lancer le mouvement*, to launch a (new) tempo.

lancio, con (It.) With verve, flinging.

Ländler (G.) A dance similar to a slow waltz.

lang, lange, langer (G.) Long, long-lasting, e.g., *lange Pause*, long rest.

langsam (G.) Slow. Also, langsamer, slower.

languendo (It.) Weak, faint, languishing. Also, languido.

languidez (Port.) Languor,

listlessness, weakness.

languido (It.) Languishing, weak, limp.

languissament (F.) Languishing. Also, languissante, avec langueur.

largamente (It.) Broadly. Also, con larghezza.

largando (It.) Becoming broader, slowing down.

large (F.) Broad, full, fairly slow. Also, largement.

larghetto (It.) A slow tempo, not quite as slow as LARGO.

largo (It.) Slow, solemn, sustained, a tempo slower than LENTO but not as slow as GRAVE.

larigot (F.) In organs, a foundation rank of diapason pipes which sound two octaves and one fifth higher than the keys played. Also, nineteenth.

las (Sp.) The.

las, lasse (F.) Tired, weary. Also, lassé.

lasciare (It.) To let, to allow, e.g., *lasciare vibrare*, let sound (continue to sound).

lassen (G.) To let, to allow, e.g., *vibrieren lassen*, let sound (continue to sound).

lässig (G.) Slow, lackadaisical.

lastend (G.) Weighty, ponderous.

Laune, mit (G.) (1) In a good humor. (2) Ill-tempered, peevish.

launig (G.) Humorous, droll.

launisch (G.) Moody, capricious, changeable, ill-tempered.

laut (G.) Loud.

Laute (G.) Lute.

lauter (G.) Louder.

le (F., It.) The.

lebendig (G.) Lively.

lebhaft (G.) Animated, lively. Also, **lebhafter**, livelier.

légal (F.) Strict, e.g., *mouvement légal*, strict tempo.

legatissimo (It.) As LEGATO as possible.

legato (It.) Smooth, even, without any break between notes. Also, **leg.**

légendaire (F.) Legendary.

léger (F.) Light, quick. Also, **légèrement, avec légèreté.**

leggiadro (It.) Graceful, elegant, light.

leggierissimo (It.) As lightly and nimbly as possible. Also, **leggieriss.**

leggiero (It.) Lightly, nimbly. Also, **leggero, con leggerezza.**

legni (It.) The woodwind section.

legno, col (It.) Playing with the wood (stick) of the bow.

legnoso (It.) Stiff, wooden.

leicht (G.) Light, airy.

leichthin (G.) Light, airy, flippant.

leidenschaftlich (G.) Passionately. Also, **mit Leidenschaft.**

leiernd (G.) Droning, monotonous.

leise (G.) Soft. Also, **leiser,** softer.

lejanía, come en (Sp.) As if from a distance, faraway.

lejano (Sp.) Distant, soft.

lent (F.) Slow. Also, **lentement, avec lenteur.**

lentamente (It.) Slowly.

lento (It., Sp.) A slow tempo.

lento epico (It.) Slow and stately.

les (F.) The.

lesto (It.) Agile, lively.

letargico (It.) Torpid, lethargic.

leuchtend (G.) Glowing, luminous.

levare (It.) To take off (organ stops, mutes). Also, **levate, si levano.**

leve (Sp., Port.) Light. Also, (Port.) **com leveza.**

lezioso (It.) Affected, mincing. Also, **lezosamente.**

L.H. (G.) Short for left hand.

libero (It.) Freely. Also, **liberamente.**

libre (F.) Free, unrestrained. Also, **librement.**

libro aperto, a (It.) At sight, sightreading.

licenza, con (It.) Freely, at the performer's discretion. Also, **con alcuna licenza**, with some freedom.

lié (F.) Tied, bound, LEGATO.

liebenswürdig (G.) Amiable, pleasant, charming.

lieblich (G.) Lovely, sweet, melodious.

liegen lassen (G.) Keep down, e.g., *Pedal liegen lassen*, keep pedal depressed.

lieto (It.) Gay, joyful. Also, **lietamente.**

lieve (It.) Light, easy. Also, **lievemente.**

ligado (Sp.) (1) Same as LEGATO. (2) Ligature.

ligar (Sp.) To tie together, to bind.

ligero (Sp.) Light, rapid.

limpide (F.) Clear, transparent.

limpido (It.) Clear, transparent.

linke Hand (G.) Left hand. Also, **L.H.**

lirico (It.) (1) Pertaining to opera, e.g., *artista lirico*, opera singer. (2) Lyrical, poetic.

lírico (Sp.) Lyrical, songlike. Also, **con lirismo.**

liscio (It.) Smooth, even, regular.

lispelnd (G.) Lisping, whispering, murmuring.

lisse (F.) Smooth, polished.

l'istesso (It.) See ISTESSO.

liuto (It.) Lute.

liviano (Sp.) Light, fleeting, frivolous.

lleno (Sp.) In organs, a mixture stop.

lo (It., Sp.) The.

locker (G.) Loose, gay, easy.

loco (It.) Return to normal position (after OTTAVA).

loin (F.) Distant, soft. Also, **lointain.**

lontanando (It.) Fading into the distance.

lontano (It.) Far-off,, remote. Also, **come in lontananza,** as if from a distance, **da lontano,** from a distance.

los (Sp.) The.

losbrechen (G.) Burst out, break forth. Also, **losbrechend.**

lourd (F.) Weighty, strong. Also, **lourdement, avec lourdeur.**

louré (F.) (1) In bowing, a LEGATO but with emphasis on each note. (2) Sounding continuosly, like a bagpipe drone.

lucide (F.) Clear, limpid.

luftig (G.) Light, airy.

Luftpause (G.) Pause for breath, either literally or figuratively.

lugubre (1) (It.) Dismal, dark, sad. (2)(F.) Mournful.

luisant (F.) Glittering, shimmering.

lumineux (F.) Clear, luminous.

luminoso (It.) Bright, shining, clear.

lunga, lungo (It.) Long, sustained, e.g., *pausa lunga*, rest, fermata. Also, (pl.) **lunghe, lunghi.**

lusingando (It.) Caressing, alluring.

lusinghiero (It.) Flattering, pleasing, caressing.

lustig (G.) Merry, cheerful.

luttuoso (It.) Doleful, sad.

lyrique (F.) Sweetly singing, melodious.

lyrisch (G.) Same as LYRIQUE.

M

ma (It.) But, e.g., *piano ma ben marcato*, soft but well accented.

mächtig (G.) (1) Powerful, loud. (2) Very, considerably, e.g., *mächtig bewegt*, quite lively.

maestoso (It.) With dignity, nobly. Also, **con maestà.**

maggiore (It.) Major.

magico (It.) Magical, enchanting.

mailloche (F.) Mallet, stick.

main droite (F.) Right hand. Also, **m.d.**

main gauche (F.) Left hand. Also, **m.g.**

mais (F.) But.

majestätisch (G.) Stately.

majestueux (F.) Stately, majestic. Also, **majestueusement, avec majesté.**

majestuoso (Sp.) Same as MAESTOSO.

majeur (F.) Major.

malice, avec (F.) Spitefully,

slyly, mischievously.

malinconico (It.) Melancholy, gloomy. Also, **con malinconia.**

malizioso (It.) Cunning, malicious, mischievous. Also, **con malizia.**

mancando (It.) Becoming softer, fading.

maniera (It.) Style, manner.

mano (It., Sp.) Hand, e.g. (It.), *mano destra*, right hand, *mano sinistra*, left hand.

marc. (It.) Short for MARCATO.

marcado (Port., Sp.) Marked, pronounced, same as MARCATO.

marcata (It.) Mark, emphasize, e.g., *marcata il basso*, emphasize the bass (part), *marcata la melodia (il canto)*, emphasize the melody.

marcatissimo (It.) As MARCATO as possible. Also, **marcatiss.**

marcato (It.) Accented, stressed. Also, **marcando, marc.**

marche (F.) March. Also, **marche funèbre**, funeral march.

märchenhaft (G.) Fairylike, fanciful.

marcia (It.) March, e.g., *alla marcia funebre*, like a funeral march, *alla marcia*, in march time.

marciale (It.) Marchlike, martial.

markiert (G.) Accented, same as MARCATO.

markig (G.) Vigorous.

marqué (F.) Marked, accented, emphasized, same as MARCATO. Also, **marquez**, emphasize, e.g., *marquez le chant*, emphasize the melody.

marschmässig (G.) In march style.

Marschzeitmass (G.) March tempo. Also, **Marschtempo**.

martelé (F.) (1) In bowing, heavy, detached up-and-down strokes, played by releasing each bow stroke suddenly, and using the area between the middle and the point of the bow. (2) In piano playing, etc., a forceful, detached effect, created by releasing the keys suddenly.

martellato (It.) Same as MARTELÉ (1).

marziale (It.) Martial, military.

mas (Sp.) But.

más (Sp.) More, most, e.g., *a más correr*, as fast as possible.

más bien (Sp.) Rather, quite.

maschio (It.) Manly.

más que (Sp.) More than, but only, even if.

massiccio (It.) Solid, heavy.

mässig (G.) (1) Moderately, e.g., *mässig bewegt*, moderately lively. (2) A moderate tempo, same as MODERATO.

matices, sin (Sp.) Without shading, without emphasis. Also, **sin matiz**.

maxixando (Port.) Like a maxixe (the Brazilian dance).

m.d. (F., It.) Right hand.

meccanico (It.) Mechanical, without expressing emotion. Also, **meccanicamente**.

méchamment (F.) Spitefully, mischievously.

méchant (F.) Wicked, malicious.

medesimo (It.) The same, e.g., *al medesimo tempo*, at the same tempo.

media (Sp.) Moderate, e.g., *a media fuerza*, with moderate loudness.

media vozi, a (Sp.) Half-voice.

medio fuerte (Sp.) Moderately loud.

medir (Sp.) Measure, meter.

meditabondo (It.) Thoughtful, reflective. Also, **meditando.**

meditativo (It.) Meditative, thoughtful.

mehr (G.) More.

melancholisch (G.) Sad.

melancólico (Sp.) Sad, gloomy. Also, **melancolía.**

mélancolique (F.) Sad, mournful, plaintive.

melodia (It.) Melody.

melodia populare (It.) Folksong.

melodico (It.) Melodic, tuneful.

Melodie (G.) Melody.

mélodique (F.) Melodious, tuneful, songlike. Also, **mélodieux.**

mélopée (F.) Chant, intonation, recitative.

même (F.) Same, e.g., *même mouvement*, same tempo.

menaçant (F.) Threatening,

foreboding.

meno (It.) Less, e.g., *meno adagio*, less slow (faster), *meno piano*, less soft (louder), *meno mosso*, less movement (slower).

menos (Sp.) Less, least.

Menschenstimme (G.) In organs, same as VOX HUMANA.

meravigliato (It.) Astonished, amazed.

mesto (It.) Sad, mournful. Also, **mestamente.**

mesure (F.) (1) Measure, bar. (2) Time, meter, e.g., *battre la mesure*, beat time.

mesuré (F.) (1) In strict time. Also, **en mesure.** (2) Measured, deliberate, moderate.

metà, la (It.) Half.

metales (Sp.) Brass section.

metallico (It.) Metallic, with a tinny sound.

metallo (It.) Vocal timbre, tone.

metá strada, a (It.) Halfway between.

métre de Maelzel (F.) Refering to the beat marked by a Maelzel metronome.

metrum (L.) Meter.

mettez (F.) Put, place, use; in organ music, to draw a stop. Also, **mettez les sourdines,** use the mutes.

mezzo, mezza (It.) Medium, half, e.g., *mezzo forte (mf),* moderately loud, softer than forte, *mezzo piano (mp),* moderately soft, louder than piano but less loud than mezzo forte, *mezza voce,* half voice.

mf (It.) Short for MEZZO forte.

m.g. (F.) Left hand.

mi (F., It., Sp.) The note or key of E, e.g., (F.) *clarinette en Mi^b,* E-flat clarinet.

minaccioso (It.) Threatening, menacing. Also, **minaccevole.**

minim (Brit.) Half note.

minore (It.) Minor.

mismo (Sp.) Same.

misterioso (It.) Mysterious, secretive.

mistico (It.) Mystical, spiritual.

misura (It.) Meter, beat, e.g., *senza misura,* not in strict time, *alla (con) misura,* in strict time, *misura binaria,* duple meter.

misurato (It.) Measured, moderate, in strict time.

mit (G.) With.

mite (It.) Gentle, moderate.

mi-voix, à (F.) Half-voice, softly, in an undertone.

mobile (It.) Changeable, capricious.

mod. (It.) Short for MODERATO.

moderado (Sp.) A moderate tempo, MODERATO.

moderato (It.) A moderate tempo, neither fast nor slow.

modéré (F.) At a moderate tempo. Also, **modérément.**

modificazioni, senza (It.) Without changes, as written.

modo (It.) Manner, style, e.g., *in modo di ballo,* in dance style.

modo de, a (Sp.) In the style of.

modo ordinario, in (It.) Play in the customary way, in normal position (fingering, bowing). Also, **modo ord.**

moëlleux (F.) Soft, mellow.

möglich (G.) Possible, e.g., *so laut als (wie) möglich,* as loud as possible.

moins (F.) Less.

moins, au (F.) At least.

moins encore (F.) Still less.

moins que (F.) Less than.

moitié (F.) Half.

moll (G.) Minor, e.g., *A-moll*, A minor.

molle (It.) Soft, languid. Also, mollemente.

mollezza, con (It.) Delicately.

molto (It.) Very, much, e.g., *molto allegro*, very fast. Also, di molto, very, extremely.

momentaneamente (It.) Momentarily.

monotamente (It.) Very evenly, without much expression.

monoton (G.) Monotonous, droning.

monotone (F.) Monotonous, very even.

monotonía, con (Sp.) Monotonously. Also, monótono.

montant (F.) Becoming louder.

montre (F.) In organs, a name for visible principal pipes that actually sound (rather than designed merely for appearance).

moqueur (F.) Jeering, mocking.

morbido (It.) Soft, delicate. Also, morbidamente.

morboso (It.) Morbid.

mordant (F.) Biting, sharp.

mordente (It.) (1) Biting, pungent. (2) An ornament (the mordent).

morendo (It.) Fading away.

mormorando (It.) Murmuring, whispering, rustling. Also, mormorevole, mormorato, come un mormorio.

morne (F.) Gloomy, sad.

mosso (It.) Moved, agitated, e.g., *più mosso*, more moved (faster), *meno mosso*, slower. Also, moto.

moto, con (It.) Somewhat lively, not too slowly, e.g., *andante con moto*, moderately slow but not too slow.

mourant, en (F.) Dying away, becoming faint.

mouvement (F.) (1) Tempo, e.g., *mouvement du début*, original tempo, *au mouvement*, return to (previous) tempo. Also mouv^t. (2) Section (movement) of a sonata, symphony, etc.

mouvementé (F.) Excited, restless.

mouvement légal (F.) Strict tempo.

movendo (It.) Moving along, faster.

movido (Sp.) Moving along, rapid.

movimento (It.) (1) Tempo, e.g., *lo stesso movimento*, the same tempo. (2) Section (movement) of a work.

movimiento (Sp.) (1) Tempo, time. (2) Motion, movement.

moyen, moyenne (F.) Average, medium, moderate.

mp (It.) Short for MEZZO piano.

m.s. (It.) Left hand.

mucho (Sp.) Much, very.

müde (G.) Weary, exhausted. Also, **Müdigkeit.**

muet, muette (F.) Silent, mute.

muito (Port.) Much, a great deal, very.

mujer (Sp.) Female, e.g., *mujer voz*, female voice.

Mund (G.) Mouth.

munter (G.) Cheerful, merry.

muovere un poco (It.) Keep going, keep moving.

murmuré (F.) Murmured, whispered. Also, **comme un murmure.**

musette (F.) (1) Bagpipe. (2) In organs, a moderately soft solo reed stop.

muta (It.) In timpani and harp parts, indication for change of tuning.

mutamento (It.) Change, alteration, e.g., *senza mutamenti una corda*, without releasing the una corda (soft) pedal.

mutazione, registro di (It.) Mutation stop.

mutig (G.) Bold, spirited.

muy (Sp.) Very much, e.g., *muy sentido*, very eloquent.

mystérieux (F.) Mysterious. Also, **mystérieusement.**

mystique (F.) Mystical, otherworldly, ethereal.

mystisch (G.) Mystical.

N

nach (G.) (1) After. (2) Behind. (3) In the manner of, according to, e.g., *nach Bedürfniss*, according to the performer's discretion.

nachdenklich (G.) Thoughtful, meditative.

Nachdruck, mit (G.) Emphatically, firmly, vigorously. Also, **nachdrücklich.**

nachgeben (G.) Slacken, slow down. Also, **nachgiebiger,** still slower.

nachlassend (G.) Slackening, slowing down and/or diminishing.

Nachschlag (G.) Ornament ending a trill, e.g., *ohne Nachschlag*, trill performed without the concluding ornament.

Nachthorn (G.) In organs, an important foundation rank, often (though not always) consisting of stopped pipes.

nächtlich (G.) Dark, gloomy.

nach und nach (G.) Little by little, gradually, e.g., *nach und nach am Steg*, gradually play near (nearer) the bridge.

näherkommend (G.) Approaching, coming closer.

naïf, naïve (F.) Simple, artless. Also, **naïvement.**

narquois (F.) Cunning, sly.

narrante (It.) Recounting, telling.

narrativo (It.) Narrative.

nasard (F.) In organs, a rank of pipes that sound one octave and a fifth higher than the keys played. Also, **nazard,** (G.) **Nasat, octave quint, open twelfth, twelfth.**

Nase, aus der (G.) A nasal tone. Also, **durch die Nase, näselnd.**

naturel (F.) Natural, normal.

natürlich (G.) Natural, simple, artless.

nazard (F.) Same as NASARD.

Nebenstimme (G.) Secondary voice (part) or melodic line.

neckisch (G.) Playful, arch.

negra (Sp.) Quarter note.

nel, nell', nella, nello (It.) In the, inside, within, at, on, to.

ne–pas (F.) Do not, e.g., *ne hâtez pas*, do not hurry (not too fast).

nera (It.) Quarter note.

nerveux (F.) Excited, impatient, agitated. Also, **nerveusement.**

nervioso (Sp.) Agitated, vigorous, energetic.

nervös (G.) Agitated, excited, fidgety.

nervoso (It.) Restless, agitated. Also, **nervosamente.**

net (F.) Clearly, plainly, distinctly. Also, **nettement.**

netto (It.) Same as NET. Also, **nettamente.**

neu (G.) New, anew, again.

neutralmente (It.) Even and simple, rhythmically and dynamically neutral.

niaisement (F.) Foolishly.

nicht (G.) Not., e.g., *nicht zu langsam*, not too slow.

niente (It.) Nothing, e.g., *estinguendosi al niente*, dying away to nothing (no sound).

no (Sp.) Not, e.g., *no mucho*, not too much.

nobilmente (It.) Dignified, stately. Also, **nobile, con nobile, con nobilità.**

nobleza, con (Sp.) Nobly, with dignity.

noch (G.) Still, yet, e.g., *noch lauter*, still louder.

noch einmal (G.) Once more, again.

noire (F.) Quarter note.

non (F., It.) No, (do) not, e.g., (It.) *non ritardare*, do not slow down.

nonchalamment (F.) Carelessly, easily. Also, **avec nonchalance.**

normal (G.) Same as NORMALE.

normale (It.) Indication to return to normal tuning, pitch, or octave, after scordatura, harmonics, etc. Also, **suono normale.**

nostalgico (It.) Longingly.

nostalgique (F.) Nostalgic, sentimental.

note blanche (F.) (1) Half note. (2) Occasionally, white key (on a keyboard instrument).

note noir (F.) Quarter note. (2) Occasionally, black key (on a keyboard instrument).

nourri, bien (F.) With a rich, full tone.

nouveau, de (F.) Again.

nuance (F.) Shading, variety of intonation.

nuance, sans (F.) Very uniform, without shading.

nuovo, di (It.) Again.

O

o (1) (It., Sp.) Or. (2) (Port.)
The.

ob. (G., It.) Short for oboe(s).

obbligato (It.) In baroque
music, an essential part. In
some 19th-century music, an
optional part.

oben (G.) Above, e.g., *wie (als)
oben*, as above, as before.

obere (G.) (1) Upper (voice-
part, manual, etc.). (2) Above.

Oboe (G.) Oboe.

oboe d'amore (It.) (1) Baroque
wind instrument, an alto
oboe. (2) In organs, a soft 8-
foot manual reed stop.

occore (It.) As needed.

octavin (F.) (1) Piccolo. (2) An
organ stop. Also, **piccolo.**

od (It.) Or.

oder (G.) Or, or else.

offen (G.) Open, unstopped.

Offenflöte (G.) In organs, an
open flute stop.

ogni (It.) Every, e.g., *pedale ad
ogni accordo*, pedal on every
chord.

ohne (G.) Without, e.g., *ohne
Pedal*, without pedal.

oíble (Sp.) Audible.

oiseau, comme un (F.) Like a
bird.

Oktavflöte (G.) Piccolo.

ombre, dans l' (F.) In the
background. Also, **à l'ombre.**

ondeggiando (It.) (1) Gently
rocking. Also, **ondeggiante.**
(2) In violin music, a wavery
tremolo, or vibrato [see
VIBRATO (1)].

ondoyant (F.) Flowing, undulating. Also, **ondulé.**

ondulado (Sp.) Rippling.

ondulando (It.) Rippling. Also,
ondulato.

ongarese, all' (It.) In Hungar-
ian (gypsy) style.

op. (L.) Short for OPUS.

opaco (It.) Dull, heavy.

opp. (It.) Short for OPPURE.

opprimente (It.) Oppressive,
burdensome, crushing.

oppure (It.) Or else, indicating
an alternative (usually easier)
version. Also **opp.**

opus (L.) Work. Also, **op.**

orageux (F.) Tempestuous.

oramai (It.) From now on, henceforth.

ordinario (It.) As usual, customary. Also, d'ordinario, in modo ordinario.

órgano (Sp.) Organ.

órgano de campanas (Sp.) Glockenspiel.

organo pleno (L.) Full organ.

Orgel (G.) Organ.

orgoglioso (It.) Haughty, proud, boastful.

orgue (F.) Organ.

orgueil, sans (F.) Without pride.

orlo, all' (It.) At the rim (of a drum, etc.).

orribile (It.) Loathsome, terrifying.

oscuro (It.) Dark, unclear.

osservato (It.) Closely observed, as written. Also, stile osservato, in strict style.

ossessivo (It.) Obsessed.

ossia (It.) Or, or else, indicating an alternative version.

ostinato (It.) A steady bass accompaniment, repeated over and over. Also, basso ostinato.

ôter (F.) Remove, stop using (organ stops, mutes, etc.). Also, ôtez.

ottava (It.) (1) Principal (organ stop). (2) Octave, usually meaning an octave higher or lower in pitch. Also, 8va, 8a, 8.

ottava alta (It.) One octave higher. Also, all'ottava, all' 8va, ottavina.

ottava bassa (It.) One octave lower.

ottaviante (It.) Overblowing (wind instrument) at the octave.

ottavino (It.) (1) Piccolo. (2) Soprano clarinet. (3) A small virginal (type of harpsichord).

ottetto (It.) Octet.

ottoni (It.) Brass section.

ou (F.) Or, or else.

ouvert (F.) (1) Open, unstopped. (2) Full-toned.

ouvert à moitié (F.) Half-open.

ovvero (It.) Or else, indicating an alternative version.

P

p (It.) Short for PIANO.

pabellon (Sp.) Bell (of horns, etc.), e.g., *pabellon en alto*, bells raised up.

pacato (It.) Calm, tranquil.

padiglione (It.) Bell (of trumpet, horn), e.g., *padiglioni in aria*, with bells up.

paisible (F.) Quiet, calm. Also, **paisiblement.**

palma, con la (Sp.) With the palm (of the hand).

palpitant (F.) Panting, quivering, fluttering.

palpitante (It.) Pulsating.

pandereta (Sp.) Tambourine.

panno (It.) A piece of cloth used to muffle a drum.

parejo (Sp.) Even, smooth.

parlando (It.) (1) In vocal music, a style approximating speech, usually in rapid tempo. (2) In instrumental music, in an expressive, declamatory style.

parlato (It.) (1) Spoken. (2) Same as parlando [see PARLANDO (1)].

parlé (F.) Spoken, speechlike.

parodia, con (It.) Parodying.

Parodie, mit (G.) Parodying, burlesquing.

part (F.) Part, voice. Also, **partie.**

parte (It.) (1) Voice-part, part. (2) Section.

parte, colla (It.) Follow the soloist's part, especially with regard to tempo.

partition (F.) Score.

Partitur (G.) Score.

pas, au (F.) At a walking pace, moderately slow.

pas à pas (F.) Step by step, gradually.

pasión, con (Sp.) With great feeling. Also, **pasionero.**

passionato (It.) Impassioned, very expressive. Also, **con passione.**

passionné (F.) Fervent, passionate, heartfelt. Also, **avec passion, passionnément.**

pastorale (It.) In pastoral style.

pastoso (It.) Flowing, euphonious, with a mellow tone.

patètico (It.) With great emotion.

pathétique (F.) Same as PATÈTICO.

pathetisch (G.) Same as PATÈTICO. Also, **mit Pathos.**

Pathos, ohne (G.) Without feeling, unsentimental.

Pauken (G.) Timpani.

paume (F.) Palm (of the hand).

pauroso (It.) Timid, fearful.

pausa (It., Sp.) Rest, e.g., (It.) *pausa di bianca*, half rest.

pause (F.) Rest.

Pause (G.) Rest, e.g., *halbe Pause*, half rest, *viertel Pause*, quarter rest.

pavillon (F.) Bell (of wind instruments), e.g., *pavillons en (á) l'air*, with the bells raised.

peccaminoso (It.) Sinful.

ped. (It.) Short for PEDALE (1), (3). In piano music, usually the damper (right) pedal.

Pedal (G.) Pedal.

pedale (It., Sp.) (1) Pedal (of organ, piano, harp, etc. Also, **ped.** (2) Pedal point. (3) In organ music, indication to use pedals only. Also, **ped.**

pédale (F.) Pedal (of organ, piano, etc.).

pedale celeste (It.) Damper pedal.

pédale de gauche (F.) Soft (una corda) pedal.

pedale del forte (It.) Sustaining (damper) pedal.

pedale doppio (It.) Double the part (in octaves) on the pedal.

Pedalgebrauch, mit (G.) Using the pedal, with pedal.

Pedalwechsel (G.) Raise and depress pedal.

peine, à (F.) Hardly, scarcely.

penaud (F.) Sheepish, bashful, embarrassed.

pendant (F.) During.

pendelnd (G.) Swinging, oscillating.

pénétrant (F.) Keen, acute, sharp.

penetrante (It.) Acute, piercing.

penosamente (It.) Painfully, with difficulty, haltingly.

pensieroso (It.) Thoughtful, serious, solemn. Also, **pensoso.**

pensif, pensive (F.) Thoughtful.

pequeño, pequeña (Sp.) Little, small, brief, e.g., *pausa pequeña*, short rest.

per (It.) By, through, for.

perçant (F.) Piercing, penetrating.

percosso (It.) Struck, clashed.

percussione (It.) Percussion section.

percussivo (It.) Percussive, heavy.

percutant (F.) Explosive, percussive, forceful. Also, **percuté.**

percutido (Sp.) Struck, hammered, percussive.

perd. (It.) Short for PERDENDO.

perdant, en se (F.) Same as PERDENDO.

perdendo (It.) Dying away. Also, **perd., perdendosi.**

perdiéndose (Sp.) Same as PERDENDO. Also, **perdiéndosi.**

perdutamente (It.) Desperately, wildly.

perfido (It.) Also, **con perfidia.** (1) Treacherously. (2) Persistent repetition of a figure.

però (It.) Nevertheless, however still, yet.

perpetuo (It.) Constant, perpetual, e.g., *moto perpetuo*, perpetual motion.

persiflierend (G.) Bantering, jesting, jocose.

pesado (Sp.) Heavy, slow, deliberate.

pesamment (F.) Same as PESADO.

pesant (F.) Same as PESADO.

pesante (It.) Weighty, ponderous, dull. Also, **pesantemente, con pesantezza.**

pesato (It.) Weighed, pondered. Also, **pesatamente.**

petite flûte (F.) Piccolo.

petite nasard (F.) In organs, a soft diapason or principal stop on the manuals.

petite trompette (F.) In organs, a moderately loud reed stop. Also, **echo trumpet.**

pettegolo (It.) Gossiping, tattling.

petulante (It.) Brash, conceited.

petulanza, con (It.) With arrogance, impertinently, pertly.

peu (F.) Little, a little. Also, **un peu.**

peu à peu (F.) Little by little, gradually.

peu pres, à (F.) Nearly, almost.

pezzo (It.) Piece, section. Composition.

pfeifend (G.) Whistling.

pfiffig (G.) Crafty, artful.

Phantasieenmässig (G.) Like a fantasy.

Phantastisch (G.) Fanciful, imaginative.

phlegmatisch (G.) Slow-moving, phlegmatic.

phrasé (F.) Phrased.

phrasiert (G.) Phrased.

piacere, a (It.) Freely, at will, at the performer's discretion, especially with regard to tempo.

piacevole (It.) Pleasing, agreeable, graceful.

pianamente (It.) Smoothly, evenly.

piangendo (It.) Weeping.

pianissimo (It.) Very soft. Also, *pp, ppp.*

piano (It.) Soft. Also, *p.*

piatti (It.) Cymbals. Also, **piattiturchi.**

piccante (It.) Sharp, pointed.

picchiettato (It.) Same as PIQUÉ (2).

piccolo (It.) (1) Small. (2) In organs, an important flute stop.

pieghevole (It.) Flexible, accommodating.

piena (It.) Full, e.g., *piena voce,* full voice.

pièno (It.) (1) Full, same as PIENA. (2) Referring to diapason stops (of organs).

pietoso (It.) (1) Pitiful, wretched. (2) Loving, devoted.

pigrizia, con (It.) Lazily, idly.

pincé (F.) (1) Stiff, prim, mannered. (2) Plucked, same as PIZZICATO. Also, **pincer.**

piqué (F.) (1) A short, quickly released note, similar to STACCATO. (2) In bowing, short detached notes produce without changing the direction of the bow.

pist. (It.) Short for cornet(s).

più (It.) More, e.g., *più andante,* slower, *più forte,* louder.

più tosto (It.) Also **piuttosto.** (1) More quickly. (2) Rather, somewhat.

pizzicato (It.) Plucked. Also, **pizz.**

placabile (It.) Soothing, mild.

placare (It.) To grow calm.

placido (It.) Calm, tranquil.

plaintif (F.) Mournful, plaintive. Also, **plaintivement.**

planer le chant, laissez (F.) Let the melody stand out.

plaqué (F.) Indication for notes of a chord to be played simultaneously (rather than in succession, as an arpeggio).

platillos (Sp.) Cymbals.

plat paume, à (F.) With the flat palm (of the hand).

plein, pleine (F.) Full, loud.

pleine sonoritè, en (F.) With a full sound.

plein jeu (F.) In organs, an important mixture stop made up of principal pipes.

pleno (It.) See PIÈNO (1).

pleurant, en (F.) Weeping, lamenting.

plötzlich (G.) Suddenly.

plus (F.) (1) More. (2) Also. See also PLUS, LE.

plus, le (F.) The most, e.g., *le plus vite possible*, as fast as possible.

plus encore (F.) Still more, e.g., *plus encore vif*, still livelier.

plus en plus, de (F.) More and more.

plus haut, comme (F.) As above, as before.

plus que (F.) More than.

plûtot (F.) Rather, quite.

pochissimo (It.) As little as possible. Also, **pochiss.**

poco (It., Sp.) Little, a bit. Also, (It.) **un po'.**

poco a poco (It., Sp.) Little by little, gradually.

poco meno (It.) A little less, (fast).

poco più (It.) A little more, e.g., *poco più mosso*, a little faster.

poderoso (Sp.) Powerful, loud.

poesia (It.) Lyrical.

poetico (It.) Poetic, lyrical.

poggiato (It.) Supported, leaning against.

poi (It.) Then, thenceforth, afterward.

poignant (F.) Heartfelt.

pointe, à la (F.) With the point of the bow.

pointu (F.) Sharp, shrill.

polacca, alla (It.) In Polish style (of a mazurka, etc.).

pollice, col (It.) With the thumb.

Pommer (G.) In organs, same as GEDECKTPOMMER.

Pomp, mit (G.) Same as POMPA, CON.

pompa, con (It.) With pomp, stately, grandiose.

pompeux, pompeuse (F.) Stately, solemn.

pomphaft (G.) Grandiose, showy, pompous.

pompös (G.) Magnificent, splendid.

pomposo (It.) Stately, majestic.

ponctué (F.) Punctuated, accented, marked.

ponticello, sul (It.) Close to the bridge (of violins, etc.), producing a nasal, brittle tone. Also, **sul pont.**

popular (Sp.) Popular, folklike, e.g., *con sentimiento popular*, in the style of folk music.

portamento (It.) A glide from one note to another.

portando la voce (It.) Carrying the voice over.

portato (It.) Half-staccato.

portez (F.) Hold, carry over, tie.

portez la voix (F.) In singing, gliding from one note to the next, in a continuous sound. Also, **port de voix.**

Portunalflöte (G.) In organs, same as BORDUNALFLÖTE.

Posaune (G.) (1) Trombone. Also, **Pos.** (2) In organs, an important chorus reed stop whose tone is much like the orchestral trombone's.

posément (F.) Sedate, stately.

positif (F.) Positive organ (or choir organ).

position naturelle (F.) Normal position (bowing). Also, **position ordinaire.**

possibile (It.) Possible, e.g., *il più presto possibile*, as fast as possible.

possierlich (G.) Droll, clowning, comical.

pouce, avec le (F.) With the thumb.

pourtant (F.) However, even so, nevertheless.

poussez (F.) Up-bow.

pp (It.) Short for pianissimo. Also, *ppp*.

prachtvoll (G.) Splendid, magnificent.

précaution, avec (F.) Warily, cautiously.

précédent (F.) Former, foregoing, preceding.

precipitado (Sp.) Hasty, abrupt.

precipitando (It.) Rushing ahead, impetuous. Also, **precipitatissimo**, as hasty as possible.

precipitar (Sp.) Same as PRECIPITANDO.

precipité (F.) Same as PRECIPITANDO.

precipitoso (It.) Same as PRECIPITANDO.

précis (F.) Exact, precise, rather terse.

preciso (It.) Exact, very accurate, precise. Also, **con precisione**.

preghevole (It.) Pleadingly.

premier, première (F.) First. Also, **Iᵉʳ, Iᵉʳᵉ**.

prenez (F.) Take (up), e.g., *prenez petite flûte*, take up (use) the piccolo.

préparez le ton de (F.) Prepare (change to) the key of.

près de (F.) Near, nearby, e.g., *près du chevalet*, near the bridge.

près de la table (F.) (Play) close to the soundboard.

presque (F.) Almost, e.g., *presque parlé*, almost spoken, *presque rien*, hardly at all, scarcely.

pressa, sem (Sp.) Without haste.

pressando (It.) Pressing on, hurrying, accelerating. Also, **pressante, pressare**.

pressant, en (F.) Hurrying, quite fast. Also, **pressez, presser**.

prestant (F.) Diapason.

preste (F.) Very fast, agile. Also, **prestement**.

prestissimo (It.) As fast as possible.

presto (It.) Fast, faster than ALLEGRO, the fastest of the conventional tempos.

prima, primo (It., Sp.) First, principal, original, e.g., *tempo primo*, original tempo, (It.) *flauto primo*, first flute. Also, **I°, Iᵐᵃ.**

primitivo (It.) (1) Original, e.g., *tempo primitivo*, original tempo. (2) Simple, plain, crude.

principale (It.) Chief part, solo.

principio (It.) Beginning, e.g., *dal principio al fine*, from beginning to end, *come in principio*, as at the beginning.

profondo (It.) (1) Profound, deep. (2) Low-pitched.

progressivement (F.) Gradually, increasingly.

prolungando (It.) Extending, sustaining.

prononciert (G.) Pronounced, enunciated.

pronto (It., Sp.) Promptly, swiftly.

pronunziato (It.) Enunciated.

proprement (F.) Neatly, suitably.

prorompendo (It.) Bursting out.

prudentemente (It.) Cautiously, carefully.

prunkvoll (G.) Pompously, ostentatiously.

psalmodie, comme une (F.) Like a psalm, intoned. Also, **en psalmodiant.**

puente (Sp.) Bridge (of violins, etc.).

pugno (It.) Fist, meaning use the fist or hand for a percussive effect on the keyboard.

puissant (F.) Forceful, loud.

pulgar (Sp.) Thumb.

pulsando (It.) Throbbing, beating, pulsating.

pungente (It.) Biting, sharp, poignant.

punta, a (It.) With the point of the bow. Also, **a punta d'arco.**

puntato (It.) (1) Dotted, staccato. (2) A simplified arrangement.

punteado (Sp.) Plucked.

pupitre (F.) Orchestral desk.

pur (F.) Clear, straightforward.

Q

quadruple-croche (F.) Sixty-fourth note.

quanto (It.) Much, how much, as much.

quart de soupir (F.) Sixteenth rest.

quasi (It.) Almost, as if, e.g., *quasi campane*, almost like bells, *quasi niente*, almost nothing (i.e., very soft).

quatre (F.) Four, e.g., *à quatre mains*, for four hands (a keyboard duet).

quattro (It.) Four, e.g., *a quattro mani*, for four hands.

quatuor (F.) Quartet.

quaver (Brit.) Eighth note.

que (1) (F., Sp.) That, which, who, whom, etc. (2) (F.) Than, as if, whether, e.g., *moins que*, less than. (3) (Sp.) Let, allow, e.g., *que se oigu el canto*, let the melody be heard (stress the melody).

Querflöte (G.) (1) Older name for orchestral flute. (2) In organs, same as FLAUTO TRAVERSO.

questo (It.) This.

quieto (It.) Quiet, hushed.

quillio (It.) Falsetto.

quint (F.) In organs, a foundation stop that sounds a fifth higher than the keys played. Also, **fifth, gross nasard.**

quintade (F.) In organs, an important stopped metal flute stop.

quintaton (F.) An organ stop. Also (G.), **Quintatön.**

Quintaten (G.) In organs, a stopped flute stop that varies widely from organ to organ.

quintette (F.) Quintet. Also, **quintuor.**

quittez (F.) Stop, leave off. Also, **quitter.**

R

rabbia, con (It.) With fury, enraged, violent. Also, **rabbioso.**

raccontando (It.) Narrated.

raddolcendo (It.) Becoming softer.

raddoppiando (It.) Double, e.g., *radoppiando il canto*, double the vocal part (with instruments).

radieux (F.) Radiant, brilliant.

radouci (F.) Softer, gentler.

raffrenando (It.) Slowing down.

rageur, avec (F.) With furor, passionately. Also, **rageusement.**

raggiungere (It.) To reach, to attain, e.g., *raggiungere il tempo* ♩ = *150*, speed up to the tempo of 150 quarter notes per minute.

ralentir (F.) To slow down. Also, **ralentissement.**

rallentando (It.) Becoming slower. Also, **rallentare, rall.**

ramenez le mouvement (F.) Return to tempo.

Rand, auf dem (G.) At the rim (of drum).

ranimant (F.) Reviving, becoming livelier.

Rankett (G.) In organs, an important reed stop.

rapace (F., It.) Rapacious, greedy, rapid.

rapidamente (It.) Quickly.

Also, **rapido.**

rapide (F.) Fast.

rápido (Sp.) Fast.

rappresentativo (It.) (1) Expressive, illustrative. (2) Typical, representative. (3) Referring to *stile rappresentativo*, a style of recitative used in early operas as well as other vocal music from about 1600 to 1650.

rapprochant, en se (F.) Approaching, coming together.

rapsodico (It.) Rhapsodically.

rasch (G.) Quick. Also, **rascher,** faster.

Raserei, mit (G.) With frenzy, enraged. Also, **rasend.**

rasgueado (Sp.) Embellished, ornamented; in guitar music, playing flourishes.

rasquedo (Sp.) Rasping, scraping.

rassegnato (It.) Resigned, reconciled, meek. Also, **con rassegnazione.**

rasserenandosi (It.) Brightening.

rattenendo (It.) Slowing down, holding back. Also, **rattenuto.**

rauco (It.) Hoarse, strident.

rauh (G.) Rough, harsh.

rauschend (G.) (1) Rustling, murmuring. (2) Roaring, swelling.

Rauschquinte (G.) In organs, a compound stop made up of diapason ranks.

ravissement, avec (F.) Rapturously.

ravivé (F.) Revived, livelier.

ravvivando (It.) Quickening, brightening.

re (It., Sp.) The note and key of D, e.g., (It.) *tromba in re*, D trumpet. Also, (F.) **ré.**

rechte Hand (G.) Right hand. Also, **R.H.**

récit (F.) (1) Recitative. Also, **récitatif.** (2) An organ manual, in English called **swell organ.**

recit. (It.) Short for RECITATIVO.

recitando (It.) Singing.

récitant (F.) Solo voice, narrator.

recitante (It.) Declaiming, in declamatory style.

recitativo (It.) (1) Recitative. (2) In declamatory style, free in rhythm and tempo.

recité (F.) Performed as a recitative; spoken.

recueilli (F.) Meditative, contemplative.

reculant (F.) Receding, delaying.

redoblante (Sp.) Tenor drum.

redonda (Sp.) Whole note.

réduction (F.) Short score.

regagnant le Ier mouvement, en (F.) Returning to the first tempo.

regelmässig (G.) Uniform, even.

religioso (It.) Sacred, devout.

renforcer (F.) To reinforce or augment, to grow louder. Also, **renforcez.**

répétez (F.) Repeat.

répétition (F.) Rehearsal.

replica (It.) Repeat.

reprenez (F.) Resume, return to, e.g., *reprenez le mouvement*, resume tempo.

reprise (F.) A repeat.

requebrando (Sp.) Flirtatious, ingratiating.

resbalad (Sp.) Sliding, a glissando.

résigné (F.) Resigned, submissive.

résolu (F.) Determined, bold.

résonné (F.) With full sound, resounding. Also, **résonner.**

respecter le doigté (F.) Follow the fingering.

respingendo (It.) Driving back, repelling.

respiro (It.) Breath.

ressortir (F.) To emphasize.

restez (F.) Remain, stay there, usually referring to a string or finger position.

resuelto (Sp.) Resolute, determined.

retardant, en (F.) Slowing down. Also, **retardez,** slow down.

retardar (Sp.) To slow down.

retenant, en (F.) Holding back, slowing down. Also, **retenez, retenu.**

retenido (Sp.) Same as RETE-NANT. Also, **retener, reteniendo.**

retournez (F.) Return.

retranchez (F.) Cut short, suppress.

rêve (F.) Dream.

revenez (F.) Return, e.g., *revenez au mouvement,* return to tempo. Also, **revenir.**

rêveur (F.) Dreamy, pensive. Also, **rêveuse, rêveusement.**

Rezitativ (G.) Recitative. Also, **Recitatif.**

rezitativartig (G.) In the manner of a recitative.

rezitieren (G.) To recite.

rf, rfz (It.) Short for RINFORZANDO.

R.H. (G.) Short for right hand.

rhytmisch (G.) Rhythmical, lilting.

rianimando (It.) Reviving, becoming.

ricercando (It.) Searching for, trying to establish, e.g., *ricercando il ritmo,* seeking the rhythm.

ricochet (F.) Same as JETÉ.

ricordando (It.) Remembering.

rideau (F.) Curtain (of a stage).

ridendo (It.) Laughing.

rigido de movimento (It.) In strict time.

rigo (It.) Staff.

rigoglioso (It.) Exuberant, vigorous.

rigor de compasso (Port.) Strict time.

rigoroso (It.) Strictly, in strict time. Also, **con rigore (di tempo), rigorosamente.**

rigoreux (F.) Strict, precise.

rigueur (F.) Strictness, e.g., *à la rigueur*, strictly (as written), *sans rigueur*, not strictly, freely.

rilasciando (It.) Slowing down.

rilassando (It.) Relaxing, slackening, slowing down.

rilievo, in (It.) Standing out, emphasized.

rimbrottando (It.) Taunting, reproaching.

rimettendosi (It.) Renewing or resuming (an earlier tempo).

rinforzando (It.) A sudden loud accent, same as SFORZANDO. Also, **rinforzato, rinf.** *rf., rfz.*

ringhiosamente (It.) Growling, snarling.

ripetizione (It.) A repeat.

ripieni, senza (It.) The first player of each section only (first horn, first oboe, etc.).

ripieno (It.) (1) In organs, a mixture stop. (2) In a concerto grosso, the full orchestra.

ripigliando (It.) Reviving, resuming.

riposo, con (It.) Restful, peaceful.

riprendendo (It.) Resuming, returning to, e.g., *riprendendo il I° tempo*, return to the original tempo.

risentito (It.) Vigorous, lively, loud.

riservato (It.) Held back, restrained.

risoluto (It.) Boldly, decisively, vigorously.

risonante (It.) Resounding, ringing, sonorous.

risonare (It.) Also, **risuonare.** (1) To resound, to echo, to continue sounding. (2) To repeat (a note, passage, etc.).

risvegliato (It.) Revived, faster.

ritardando (It.) Becoming slower. Also, **ritardare, ritard., rit.**

ritenuto (It.) Immediately slower, held back. Also, **riten.**

ritmico (It.) Rhythmic, in strict time.

rítmico (Sp.) Rhythmic.

ritmo (It., Sp.) Rhythm.

ritmo, a gran (Sp.) Very fast.

ritornando (It.) Returning. Also, **ritornate.**

ritraendosi (It.) Representing, depicting.

riverbero (It.) Echo, reverberation.

riverso (It.) (1) Inversion. (2) Retrograde motion.

robust (G.) Sturdy, strong, firm, bold.

robustement (F.) Vigorously.

robusto (It.) Same as ROBUST.

roco (It.) Hoarse.

roh (G.) Rough, crude.

Rohr (G.) In organs, referring to various pipes that are half-covered (or half-open), e.g., **Rohrgedeckt, Rohrschalmei,** etc.

Rohrbordun (G.) In organs, a half-covered flute stop.

Rohrflöte (G.) In organs, a half-covered solo and ensemble flute stop. Also, **chimney flute.**

Rohrpommer (G.) In organs, a half-covered GEDECKTPOMMER of large scale.

rollante (It.) Rolling (like a ship).

ronde (F.) Whole note.

rondement (F.) Quickly, briskly.

roulement (F.) Drum roll.

rubato (It.) Taking a portion of the value from one note and giving it to another note (usually) within the same measure, without altering the duration of the measure as a whole. Also, **tempo rubato.**

Rückerinnerung (G.) Reminiscence.

rückkehrend (G.) Returning, reverting.

rücksichtslos (G.) Reckless, heedless, without consideration. Also, **ohne Rücksicht.**

rude (F., It.) Rough, harsh, unevenly. Also, (F.) **rudement,** (It.) **con rudezza.**

rufend (G.) Calling.

ruhelos (G.) Restless, disquieted.

ruhevoll (G.) Restful, calm.

ruhig (G.) Quiet, calm. Also, **mit Ruhe.**

ruhiger (G.) Softer.

Rührtrommel (G.) Tenor drum.

Rührung (G.) Deep feeling. Also, **rührend.**

rullo (It.) Drum roll.

rulo (Sp.) Drum roll.

rumor, como un (Sp.) Like a murmur, buzzing.

rumoroso (Sp.) Loud, rumbling.

russico, nel modo (It.) In Russian style.

rustico (It.) Rustic, plain, simple.

ruvido (It.) Rough, coarse. Also, **ruvidamente, con ruvidezza.**

rythme (F.) Rhythm.

rythmé (F.) Measured, in precise rhythm.

rythme brisé (F.) Broken rhythm, uneven.

S

saccadé (F.) Abrupt, jerky.

Saite (G.) String.

salicional (F.) An organ stop.

salmodiando (It.) Intoning, psalm-like. Also, **salmodico.**

saltando (It.) Same as SAUTILLÉ. Also, **saltato, salt.**

saltellante (It.) Skipping, tripping lightly. Also, **saltellato.**

sanft (G.) Soft, gentle.

sans (F.) Without.

sardonico (It.) Sneering, sarcastic.

sassofone (It.) Saxophone.

satanico (It.) Devilish, satanic, evil.

satirico (It.) Mocking, satirical.

satt (G.) Full, satisfied, e.g., *mit sattem Ton*, with a full tone.

Satz (G.) Movement (of a sonata, symphony, etc.).

sauté de la pointe (F.)
Bounced against the strings
with the tip of the bow.

sautillant (F.) Jerky, skipping.

sautillé (F.) In bowing, a short
rapid detached stroke, played
in the middle of the bow, that
makes the bow bounce lightly
off the string.

sauvage (F.) Wild, untamed.

saxófono (Sp.) Saxophone.
Also, **saxofón.**

sbalzare (It.) To move by
leaps, skipping, bounding.
Also, **sbalzato.**

sbeffeggiando (It.) Mocking.

sbloccata (It.) Released.

scalpitante (It.) Pounding,
galloping.

scampanatino (It.) Tinkling,
bell-like.

scandé (F.) Scanned, broken
up into separate units of
rhythm and meter, syllabic.

scandendo (It.) Ascending.

scandito, ben (It.) Pronounced
distinctly, well articulated.
Also, **scandire.**

scatenato (It.) Unleashed,
tempestuous.

scattando (It.) Bursting out.

scemando (It.) Becoming
softer.

schalkhaft (G.) Roguish, sly.

Schalltrichter (G.) Bells (of
wind instruments).

Schalmei (G.) In organs, an
important reed stop,
resembling the tone of the
medieval shawm. Also,
shawm, (F.) **chalumeau.**

scharf (G.) (1) Sharp, sudden.
(2) *cap.* In organs, same as
ACUTA.

scharrend (G.) Scratching,
scraping.

schattenhaft (G.) Subtly blend-
ed, shaded. Also, **schattig.**

schaudernd (G.) Shuddering,
trembling.

schelmisch (G.) Sly, roguish,
arch.

scherzando (It.) Playfully,
jestingly. Also, **scherzevole,
scherzoso.**

scherzhaft (G.) Playful, jocular.
Also, **scherzend.**

scherzo (It.) Referring to the
tempo and mood of a scherzo
movement, i.e., lively and
brisk.

scherzoso (It.) Playful, lively.

schiamazzando (It.) Squawking, clamoring, in a continual uproar.

schianto, come uno (It.) Like a crash or a sudden blow.

schiettamente (It.) Openly, simply, plainly. Also, **schietto.**

Schlag (G.) A stroke, a blow.

schlagen (G.) To strike, to beat, e.g., *Achtel schlagen*, beat eighth notes.

Schlagwerk (G.) Percussion section. Also, **Schlaginstrumente.**

schleichend (G.) Creeping, furtive.

schleppend (G.) Dragging, slow.

schlicht (G.) Plain, straightforward, smooth, e.g., *mit schlichtem Vortrag*, perform smoothly.

schluchzend (G.) Sobbing.

Schluss (G.) End, e.g., *bis zum Schluss*, up to the end.

Schlüssel (G.) Clef.

schmachtend (G.) Languishing, yearning.

schmeichelnd (G.) Coaxing,

flattering.

schmelzend (G.) (1) Sweet, melodious. (2) Diminishing.

schmerzlich (G.) Painful, distressed.

schmetternd (G.) (1) Loud, blaring. (2) In horn playing, a harsh, brassy tone.

Schnarrsaite (G.) Snarehead (of a snare drum).

schneidend (G.) Cutting, sharp, biting.

schnell (G.) Fast. Also, **Schnelligkeit,** speed.

schneller (G.) (1) Faster. (2) *cap.* Inverted mordent.

schnippisch (G.) Pert, snappish.

Schöngedeckt (G.) In organs, a stopped flute stop.

schreitend (G.) Striding, moving slowly and steadily.

schrittmässig (G.) Measured, even.

schroff (G.) Gruff, harsh.

schwach (G.) Weak, soft. Also, **schwächer,** softer, weaker.

Schwammschlager (G.) Sponge-headed drumstick.

schwärmerisch (G.) With enthusiasm, wild.

schwebend (G.) Light, floating.

schwelgend (G.) Voluptuous.

schwellen (G.) Swell, grow
louder. Also, schwellend.

Schweller (G.) Swell organ.
Also, Schwellwerk.

schwer (G.) Serious,
ponderous.

schweren Akzenten, mit (G.)
With heavy accents.

schwerfällig (G.) Heavy, slow.

schwermütig (G.) Melancholy,
moody.

schwindend (G.) Dying away.

Schwung, mit (G.) Lively, with
verve. Also, schwungvoll.

scintillant (F.) Sparkling,
brilliant. Also, (F., It.)
scintillante.

scioltezza, con (It.) With ease,
fluently.

sciolto (It.) Easy, unconstrained, fluent. Also,
scioltamente.

scivolando (It.) Same as
GLISSANDO. Also, scivolare sulla
tastiera, slide over the

keyboard.

scolpito (It.) Clear and distinct. Also, scolpitante.

scomparendo (It.) Disappearing, vanishing.

scoperto (It.) Exposed, bare,
clear.

scordato (It.) Out of tune, off
pitch.

scordatura (It.) Deliberate
change in tuning.

scorrendo (It.) Flowing,
gliding. Also, scorrevole.

scucito (It.) Unconnected, detached, opposite of LEGATO.

scuro (It.) Dark, gloomy.

sdegnoso (It.) Haughty,
scornful.

sdrucciolando (It.) Slippery,
sliding.

sea pueda (Sp.) As possible.

sec, sèche (F.) Drily, abruptly.
Also, avec sécheresse.

secco (It.) Plain, simple,
unadorned.

Sechzehntel (G.) Sixteenth
note.

seco (Sp.) Dry, concise.

seconda (It.) Second, e.g., *seconda volta*, second time. Also, 2da.

secondaire (F.) Secondary.

seelenvoll (G.) Soulful, heartfelt.

segno (It.) Sign, meaning the sign 𝄋 or ⊕. Thus, *al segno*, to the sign, *dal segno*, from the sign.

segreto (It.) Hidden, furtive.

segue (It.) Continue without pausing.

seguendo (It.) Following, e.g., *seguendo l'azione*, following the action (on stage).

seguidilla (Sp.) A traditional Spanish dance.

seguire il canto (It.) Follow the melody (vocal part, solo).

sehnsuchtsvoll (G.) With longing, wistful. Also, **sehnsüchtig, mit Sehnsucht.**

sehr (G.) Very, e.g., *sehr langsam*, very slow.

seizième de soupir (F.) Sixty-fourth rest.

selbe (G.) Same, e.g., *das selbe Zeitmass*, the same tempo.

selig (G.) Blissful, happy, heavenly.

selon (F.) According to.

selvaggio (It.) Wild, savage, boisterous. Also, **selvaggiamente.**

sem (Port.) Without.

semibiscroma (It.) Sixty-fourth note.

semibreve (Brit., It.) Whole note.

semicorchea (Sp.) Sixteenth note.

semicroma (It.) Sixteenth note.

semifusa (Sp.) Sixty-fourth note.

semiminima (It.) Quarter note.

semiquaver (Brit.) Sixteenth note.

semp. (It.) Short for SEMPRE.

semplice (It.) Simple, unaffected. Also, **con semplicità.**

sempre (It., Port.) Always, continually, throughout, e.g., (It.) *sempre dopo la voce*, always following the voice (vocal part).

sencillamente (Sp.) Simply, plainly. Also, **con sencillez.**

sensibile (It.) (1) Sensitive, tender. (2) The leading tone. Also, **nota sensibile.**

sentido (Sp.) Heard, audible.

sentiment (F.) Feeling, mood. e.g., *avec un sentiment émouvant*, with deep feeling.

sentimento, con (It.) With feeling. Also, **sentimentale.**

sentimiento (Sp.) (1) With feeling. (2) Sorrowful.

sentito (It.) (1) Heard. (2) Expressive, heartfelt, warm.

senza (It.) Without, e.g., *senza pedale*, without pedal.

separado (Sp.) Same as DETACHÉ.

separato (It.) Detached.

separez (F.) Separate, un-couple (in organs).

septadecima (L.) In organs, same as TIERCE.

septième (F.) In organs, a foundation rank of soft open metal pipes, which sound two octaves and a minor seventh higher than the keys played. Also, **twenty-first, flatted.**

septuor (F.) Septet.

Seraphonflöte (G.) In organs, an open flute stop. Also, **Jubalflöte.**

serein (F.) Placid, tranquil.

serenidad (Sp.) Calm, peaceful.

sereno (It.) Same as SERENIDAD. Also, **serenamente, con serenitá.**

serietà, con (It.) Seriously, earnestly, gravely. Also, **serioso.**

serrer (F.) Condense, speed up. Also, **serrez, serré, en serrant.**

sesquialtera (It.) In organs, an important mixture stop, usually made up of diapason pipes.

sestetto (It.) Sextet.

settimino (It.) Septet.

Seufzer, wie ein (G.) Like a sigh.

seul, seule (F.) Alone.

seulement (F.) Only.

severo (It.) Strict, rigid.

sf, sfz (It.) Short for SFORZANDO.

sferzante (It.) Rebuking, punishing.

sfida (It.) Defiance, e.g., *con accento di sfida*, with a defiant air.

sfiorato (It.) Touching lightly, skimming over, caressing.

sfogato (It.) (1) Let loose, freed. (2) Exhaled; in singing, very light and airy.

sfoggiando (It.) Ostentatious, lavish.

sfolgorante (It.) Flashing, brilliant.

sforzando (It.) With a strong accent. Also, **rinforzando, sforzato, sforzo, sf. sfz.**

sforzata (It.) Forced, e.g., *sforzata gaiezza*, forced gaiety.

sforzato (It.) Same as SFORZANDO.

sfp (It.) Short for sforzando piano, accented, then soft.

sfrenato (It.) Unrestrained, wild.

sfumando (It.) Fading away, gradually diminishing. Also, **sfumato.**

sgarbatamente (It.) Rudely, awkwardly.

sguaiato (It.) Rude, coarse. Also, **sguaiatamente.**

si (F., It., Sp.) The note or key of B, e.g., (It.) *tromba in Si♭*, B-flat trumpet.

sibillino (It.) Mysterious.

siciliana (It.) A Sicilian dance in 6/8 meter and fairly slow tempo.

sicurezza, con (It.) With assurance. Also, **sicuro.**

sieghaft (G.) Victorious.

siempre (Sp.) Always, constantly.

sifflant (F.) (1) Hissing, whistling. (2) Flutter tonguing.

Sifflöte (G.) In organs, a manual flute stop with a brilliant tone.

signe (F.) Sign, usually 𝄋.

sigue (Sp.) Continue without pause.

silbern (G.) Silvery, with a clear, bell-like tone.

silencio (Sp.) Rest, e.g., *silencio de negra*, quarter rest.

silenzio (It.) Silence, rest.

sillabando (It.) Pronouncing by syllables.

sillabato, ben (It.) Clearly articulated.

silofono (It.) Xylophone.

simile (It.) Similarly, in like manner. Also, **sim.**

simple (F.) Plain, simple, artless. Also, **simplement.**

sin (Sp.) Without.

sin' (It.) Up to, until.

sine (L.) Without.

singend (G.) Singing, melodious, CANTABILE. Also, singbar.

singhiozzando (It.) Sobbing, hiccupping.

singhiozzo, come un (It.) (1) Like a sob or hiccup. (2) The device of hocket.

sinistra (It.) Left (hand). Also, colla mano sinistra, m.s.

Sinn, nach dem (G.) According to the meaning of the words.

sino (It.) Up to, until. Also, sin', e.g., sin'al fine, up to the end.

sinuoso (It.) Smooth, curving.

sipario (It.) Curtain (of a stage).

sirène (F.) Siren.

slancio, con (It.) Vigorously, with dash. Also, di slancio, a brilliant attack.

slargando (It.) Slowing down.

slentando (It.) Slackening, slowing down.

slontando (It.) Withdrawing,

becoming softer.

smanioso (It.) Ardent, frenzied.

smarrito (It.) Bewildered, confused.

sminuendo (It.) Becoming softer.

smorendo (It.) Dying away.

smorfioso (It.) Affected, mincing.

smorzando (It.) Fading away. Also, smorz.

snèllo (It.) Nimble, agile, brisk.

so (G.) As, e.g., doppelt so schnell, twice as fast.

soave (It.) Gentle, sweet, delicate. Also, soavemente.,

soavissimo (It.) As sweetly (gently, delicately) as possible.

sobre (Sp.) On, over, above, e.g., sobre el puente, over the bridge.

sobresaliendo (Sp.) Emphasizing, standing out.

sobrio (Sp.) Sober, restrained.

sofferente (It.) (1) Suffering, ill. (2) Patient, enduring.

soffice (It.) Light, gentle, soft.

soffio, come un (It.) Like a breath, very light.

soffocato (It.) Smothered, damped. Also, **con voce soffocata,** with a muffled voice.

sofort (G.) Immediately, at once, e.g., *sofort anschliessen,* connect immediately (continue without pause).

soggetto (It.) Subject, theme.

sognando (It.) Dreaming, musing. Also, **sognante.**

sogno, come un (It.) Like a dream, illusive.

soigneusement (F.) Carefully, elegantly. Also, **soigneuxment, avec soin.**

soignez le son (F.) Refine the tone.

sol (F., It., Sp.) The note and key of G.

solaire (F.) Sunny, bright.

solenne (It.) Very serious, stately. Also, **con solennità.**

solennel (F.) Solemn, sedate.

solito (It.) Customary, e.g., *come al solito,* as usual.

solo (It., Port., Sp.) (1) Single, alone, a part for one per-

former. Also, (It. pl.) **soli.** (2) In organs, term for various stops of more conspicuous tone color than the average rank of the same name, e.g., **solo tibia clausa, solo tuba,** etc.

sombre (F.) Melancholy, gloomy.

sombrío (Sp.) Gloomy, somber.

somma (It.) Highest, utmost.

sommeillant (F.) Sleepy, slow.

sommesso (It.) Subdued, soft.

somnolent (F.) Drowsy, relaxed.

son (F.) Tone, sound, e.g., *à plein son,* with a full tone.

sonabile (It.) (1) Playable. (2) Sonorous, ringing, resonant.

son harmonique (F.) Harmonic (overtone).

sonido (Sp.) Sound, tone.

sonido abierto (Sp.) Same as CUIVRÉ.

sonido natural (Sp.) Natural tone; in violins, etc., open tone.

sonnacchioso (It.) Sleepy, sluggish.

sonore (F.) Resounding, loud.

sonorité (F.) Resonance, tone quality.

sonoro (It.) Resonant, full-toned. Also, **sonoramente.**

sopra (It.) Over, above, e.g., *come sopra*, as above (as before).

sordamente (It.) Muted, very soft. Also, **sordo.**

sordina (Sp.) Mute or damper.

sordino (It.) Mute or damper, e.g., *con sordini*, with mutes or damper (pedal), *senza sordini*, without mutes or damper. Also, **sord.**

sordo (Sp.) Muffled.

sorgendo (It.) Rising, emerging, becoming louder.

sorglos (G.) Carefree.

sorridente (It.) Smiling, fondly musing.

sospeso (It.) Suspended.

sospettoso (It.) Suspicious, wary, dubious.

sospirando (It.) Sighing, plaintive. Also, **sospirato.**

sostenido (Sp.) Same as SOSTENUTO.

sostenuto (It.) Sustained. Also, **sost.**

sotto (It.) Under, below.

sotto voce (It.) Softly, in a low voice.

soubasse (F.) In organs, the principal bass stop, with a big, intense tone. Also, **contra bourdon, sub bass, sub bourdon,** (G.) **Untersatz.**

soudainement (F.) Suddenly. Also, **soudain.**

souffle (F.) Breath, e.g., *dans un souffle*, in one breath, *comme un souffle*, like a breath, very light.

souffrant (F.) Suffering, grieving. Also, **avec souffrance.**

soupir (F.) (1) Quarter rest. (2) Sigh, breath, gasp.

soupirant (F.) Sighing, plaintive.

souple (F.) Flexible, smooth. Also, **souplement, avec souplesse.**

sourd (F.) Indistinct, muffled, muted. Also, **sourdement.**

sourdine (F.) Mute or damper.

soutenu (F.) Sustained, held.

sparire (It.) To fade away.

spasshaft (G.) Lively, playful.

spavalderia, con (It.) Impudently, defiantly. Also, **spavaldo.**

spaziato (It.) Ranging freely, wandering.

spazzole (It.) Brushes (used with percussion instruments). Also, **con spazzola.**

spegnendosi (It.) Dying away.

spegnere il suono (It.) To stop the sound, to become silent.

spensieratamente (It.) Thoughtlessly, freely.

speranza, senza (It.) Without hope, lacking confidence.

sperdendosi (It.) Fading away.

spianato (It.) Smooth, even, sustained.

spiccato (It.) (1) In bowing, either a light staccato or the same as SAUTILLÉ. Also, **spicc.** (2) **spiccato col legno,** a light staccato played with the stick of the bow.

spiegato (It.) With full voice and becoming louder. Also, **a voce spiegata.**

Spieler (G.) Player, performer.

spielerisch (G.) Playful, jocular.

spietato (It.) Ruthless, cruel.

spigliato (It.) Agile, nimble, graceful.

Spillflöte (G.) In organs, an open flute stop. Also, **Spindelflöte.**

Spindelflöte (G.) Same as SPILLFLÖTE.

spingendo (It.) (1) Driving ahead. (2) Up-bowing.

spirando (It.) Breathing, exhaling.

Spireflöte (G.) In organs, same as SPITZFLÖTE.

spiritoso (It.) Spirited, lively. Also, **con spirito.**

spiritu, con (L.) With spirit.

spitz (G.) (1) Sharp, biting. Also, **spitzig.** (2) *cap.* Point of the bow. Also, **an der Spitze,** with the point of the bow.

Spitzflöte (G.) In organs, an important open flute stop. Also, **Spireflöte.**

Spitzprinzipal (G.) In organs, an important foundation stop, made up of slightly conical pipes. Also, **cone diapason, Spitz diapason.**

spottisch (G.) Mocking, sarcastic.

Sprechstimme (G.) Inflected speech-like singing, with pitches only approximated.

sprezzante (It.) Haughty, disdainful. Also, **con sprezzo.**

springend (G.) Bouncing. In bowing, *mit springendem Bogen,* bouncing the bow against the strings, as in SAUTILLÉ.

spugna (It.) Sponge, e.g., *bacchette di spugna,* sponge-headed drumsticks.

squarciagola, a (It.) At the top of the voice, yelling.

squillante (It.) Blaring, pealing, shrill.

stabile (It.) Firm, steady.

staccatissimo (It.) A sharp STACCATO.

staccato (It.) Detached, with each note separated from the next and quickly released. Also, **stacc.**

staccato volante (It.) "Flying" STACCATO, in which the bow springs slightly off the string.

stammelnd (G.) Stammering, faltering.

stampfend (G.) Stamping, pounding.

stancamente (It.) Wearily, slowly, dragging. Also, **stanco,** con stanchezza.

Stange (G.) Stick of the bow, e.g., *Stange geschlagen,* bounce stick against the strings, same as LEGNO, COL.

stark (G.) (1) Strong, vigorous, loud. Also **stärker,** louder. (2) Very, e.g., *stark bewegt,* very lively.

starr (G.) Rigid, inflexible.

statico (It.) Steady, unchanging.

Steg, am (G.) On (near) the bridge.

steigernd (G.) Augmenting, becoming louder. Also, **in Steigerung.**

Stelle (G.) Place, e.g., *an der selben Stelle,* in the same place.

stendendo (It.) Slowing down.

stentando (It.) Difficult, labored, slow. Also, **stentato, stent.**

Stenthorn (G.) In organs, a loud 8-foot manual solo stop.

Stentor (G.) In organs, name for various stops that are unusually loud and powerful, e.g., **Stentorflöte, Stentor gamba,** etc.

sterbend (G.) Dying away.

steso (It.) Slow, broad.

stesso (It.) Same, e.g., *lo stesso movimento*, the same tempo.

stetig (G.) Same as STETS.

stets (G.) Continually, always, e.g., *stets arpeggieren*, continually (play) broken chords. Also, **stetig**.

Stil (G.) Style.

stile (It.) Style, e.g., *stile di recitativo*, in the style of a recitative.

still (G.) Quiet, soft.

Stimme (G.) (1) Voice, e.g., *mit erregter Stimme*, in an agitated voice. (2) Voice-part. (3) Organ stop.

stimmen (G.) (1) To tune. (2) (cap.) Voices.

Stimmung (G.) (1) Mood, e.g., *heitere Stimmung*, happy mood. (2) Tuning, e.g., *Stimmung halten*, stay in tune. (3) Pitch, key, e.g., *die selbe Stimmung*, the same key.

stinguendo (It.) Fading away.

stiracchiando (It.) Drawing out, slowing down. Also, **stirato**.

stizzoso (It.) Petulant, spiteful.

stockend (G.) Hesitating, haltingly, slackening in tempo.

stolz (G.) Stately, majestic.

straff (G.) Rigid, tense, concise.

strahlend (G.) Beaming, radiant.

strappata (It.) Plucked, strummed. Also, **strappate**, **strappato**.

strasciando (It.) Dragging. Also, **strascicamente**.

strascinando (It.) Also, **strascinare, strascinato.** (1) Drawling, drawing out, dragging. (2) A glissando or portamento, i.e., sliding from one note to another.

stravaganza, con (It.) Whimsically, fancifully. Also, **stravagante**.

straziante (It.) Anguished, tortured. Also, **straziando, con strazio.**

streichen (G.) To bow, e.g., *breit streichen*, bow broadly (with long broad strokes).

Streicher (G.) String section. Also, **Streichinstrumente**.

streng (G.) Strict, exact, e.g., *streng im Takt*, in strict tempo.

strepitoso (It.) Noisy, boisterous. Also, **con strepito**.

stretta (It.) A STRETTO passage.

stretta, alla (It.) Faster.

strette (F.) A stretto passage
(STRETTO 2).

stretto (It.) (1) Accelerated,
faster. (2) A concluding
section in faster tempo. (3) In
contrapuntal music, the
device of speeding up
imitation by the various parts.

Strich (G.) Stroke, bow stroke.

strictement (F.) Strictly, exact-
ly, e.g., *strictement en mesure*, in
strict time.

stridente (It.) Shrill, sharp,
jarring. Also, **stridulo.**

stringendo (It.) Pressing on,
hurrying, speeding up. Also,
stringente, string.

strisciando (It.) A glide from
one note to the next.

strisciata (It.) Rubbing, strok-
ing, sliding (for cymbals, etc.).

strömend (G.) Flowing.

strozzata (It.) Strangled,
choking.

strumento (It.) Musical instrument. Also, (pl.) **strumenti.**

stumm (G.) Mute, silent.

stürmisch (G.) Stormy, violent,
passionate.

Stürze (G.) Bell (of wind
instrument).

su, arco in (It.) Up-bow.

suadente (It.) Persuasive, con-
vincing.

suave (Sp.) Smooth, gentle,
soft.

sub. (It.) Short for SUBITO.

subit, subite (F.) Sudden,
suddenly.

subito (It.) Suddenly,
immediately, at once, e.g., *p.
subito*, abrupt change to soft,
volti subito, turn (the page)
fast. Also, **sub.**

súbito (Sp.) Sudden.

subtil (1) (F.) Subtle, acute. (2)
(G.) Subtle, delicate.

suelto (Sp.) Loose, free,
flowing.

suivant (F.) According to,
following.

suivez (F.) (1) Continue next
section without pause. (2)
Follow the soloist, especially
with regard to tempo.

sul, sulla, sulle (It.) On the.

suonare (It.) To sound, e.g.,
lasciar suonare, let (continue)
to sound.

suonare a fantasia (It.) Improvise.

suoni armonici (It.) Harmonics.

suoni reali (It.) Actual pitches to be sounded.

suono (It.) Musical sound, e.g., *senza suono*, without music (i.e., spoken).

suppliant (F.) Beseeching, entreating.

sur (F.) On, over, e.g., *sur la touche*, over the fingerboard.

suspirante (Sp.) Sighing, longingly.

süss (G.) Sweet, melodious.

sussurro (It.) Whisper, murmur. Also, **sussurrando, sussurrato.**

susteniendo (Sp.) Sustaining, holding, e.g., *susteniendo con los pedales*, sustain with the pedals.

svagato (It.) Absentminded, heedless.

svanendo (It.) Fading away.

svegliando (It.) Awakening, becoming agitated.

svelto (It.) Brisk, light, lively.

T

table (F.) Soundboard, belly.

tace (It.) Be silent.

tacet (L.) Be silent, marking part where instrument or voice is omitted.

tagliente (It.) Sharp, keen.

Takt (G.) (1) Measure, bar, e.g., *Pedal jeden Takt*, use pedal for each measure. (2) Beat, meter, time, e.g., *3/4 Takt*, 3/4 meter. (3) Tempo.

Takt, im (G.) In strict time. Also, *streng im Takt.*

Takt, ohne (G.) In free rhythm and time.

Takteinteilung, ohne (G.) Without being divided into measures, without bar lines.

talon, au (F.) At the frog end of the bow. Also, **du talon.**

talone, al (It.) Same as TALON, AU.

tambor con tirantes de cuerdas (Sp.) Snare drum.

tambour (F.) Drum.

tambour de Basque (F.) Tambourine.

tambourin (F.) Long drum.

tambour militaire (F.) Snare drum.

tamburo (It.) Drum.

tam-tam (F.) Gong.

tan (Sp.) As much, e.g., *tan lento sea pueda*, as slowly as possible.

tändelnd (G.) Playful, flirting.

tanto (It.) Much, so much, as much, e.g., *allegro ma non tanto*, fast but not too much so.

tänzerisch (G.) Dancelike. Also, **tanzhaft.**

Tanzzeitmass (G.) Dance tempo.

tapado (Sp.) Muffled.

tardamente (It.) Slowly, wearily.

tardo (It.) (1) Slow, serious. (2) Late, delayed. Also **tardato.**

tasto (It.) (1) Fingerboard, e.g., *sul tasto*, over (near) the fingerboard. Also, **sulla tastiera.** (2) Key (of keyboard instrument). (3) Fret.

tasto solo (It.) Bass part alone, without harmonies above it.

tautino (It.) Stubborn, bull-like.

tavola, sulla (It.) Over the belly (of violins, etc.).

t.c. (It.) Short for TRE CORDE.

Teil (G.) Part, section, e.g., *wie im ersten Teil*, as in the first part.

Tem.Iº (It.) Short for tempo primo (see PRIMA).

tema (It.) Theme, subject.

temperamentvoll (G.) Spirited, impulsive.

tempestoso (It.) Stormy, passionate.

tempête, en (F.) Tempestuous, passionate.

tempo (It.) Time, rate of speed. Also, (pl.) **tempi.**

tempo, a (It.) Return to the original tempo.

tempo di (It.) In the tempo of e.g., *in tempo di menuetto*, in the tempo of a minuet.

Tempoveränderung (G.) Change of tempo.

temps (F.) Beat.

temps, en même (F.) At the same time.

ten. (It.) Short for TENUTO.

tenacemente (It.) Constantly, tenaciously.

Tendenz zur (G.) Tending toward, e.g., *Tendenz zur Ruhe*, tending to be soft.

tendrement (F.) Tenderly, lovingly. Also, **tendre**.

tenebroso (It.) Gloomy, somber.

teneramente (It.) Tenderly, gently. Also, **tenero, con tenerezza**.

tenido (Sp.) Held, sustained.

tenu (F.) Same as TENIDO.

tenuemente (Sp.) Slightly.

tenuto (It.) Held, sustained. Also, **tenuti, ten.**

teso (It.) Taut, tight, tense.

tetro (It.) Gloomy, dark, sad.

tibia (It., L.) In organs, an 8-foot open flute stop on the manuals.

tibia clausa (L.) In organs, an important stopped flute stop.

tibia plena (L.) In organs, a loud open 8-foot flute stop.

tibia profunda (It. + L.) In organs, a very low-pitched flute stop.

tibia sylvestris (L.) In organs, same as WALDFLÖTE.

tief (G.) (1) Deep, profound. (2) Low (in pitch).

tiefgesättigt (G.) Contented.

tiefschürfender Empfindung, mit (G.) With deep emotion.

tiempo (Sp.) Tempo, rate of speed.

tierce (F.) In organs, a rank of foundation pipes that sound two octaves and a third higher than the keys played. Also, **septadecima, seventeenth.**

timbales (F., Sp.) Timpani (kettledrums).

timballi (It.) Timpani (kettledrums).

timbre (F.) Tone color.

timbro (It.) (1) Tone color. (2) The jingle of a tambourine.

timido (It.) Shy, bashful, hesitant. Also, **timidamente, con timidezza.**

timpani (It.) Kettledrums. Also, **timp.**

tirado (Sp.) Down-bow.

tirare in dietro (It.) To draw back.

tirasse (F.) Organ coupler, e.g., *sans tirasse*, pedal uncoupled.

tirata (It.) In vocal music, a slide or glide.

tirez (F.) Down-bow.

Todeslied (G.) A dirge, a lament. Also, **Todesgesang.**

todos (Sp.) All, everybody.

togliere la mano (It.) Remove the hand.

ton (F.) Tone, sound, pitch.

Ton (G.) Same as TON.

Tonart (G.) Key, tonality.

Tonleiter (G.) Scale.

tonlos (G.) Toneless, monotonous.

tonvoll (G.) Tuneful, melodious.

torbido (It.) Gloomy, murky.

tornando (It.) Returning.

torrent, en (F.) Pouring out.

torturado (Sp.) Tortured, afflicted.

tosto (It.) Fast. See also PIÙ TOSTO.

touche (F.) (1) Key (of a key-board instrument), e.g., *touche noire*, black key, *touche blanche*, white key. (2) Fingerboard of a stringed instrument, e.g., *sur la touche*, (bow) over the fingerboard.

toujours (F.) Always, constantly.

tourbillonnant (F.) Whirling.

tous, tout, toute (F.) All, every, whole.

tr. (It.) (1) Short for TRILLO. (2) Short for trumpet(s).

träge (G.) Slow, lifeless.

tragico (It.) Tragic.

traîner (F.) To drag, to hold back, to slur. Also, **traîné.**

trait (F.) A rapid passage.

tranchant (F.) Sharp, cutting.

tranquillamente (It.) Same as TRANQUILLE.

tranquille (F.) Quiet, peaceful, soft.

tranquillo (It.) Same as TRANQUILLE.

tranquilo (Sp.) Same as TRANQUILLE.

transfiguré (F.) Transfigured, changed.

trascinando (It.) Dragging, slowing down, drawing out the tone. Also, **trascinato, trascinare.**

trasfigurato (It.) Transformed, changed.

trasognato (It.) Daydreaming, half asleep.

trasparente (It.) Clear, transparent.

trasporto (It.) (1) Joyful, rapturous. (2) Transposed.

trattenuto (It.) Held, sustained, slowed down.

tratto (It.) Drawn, e.g., *tratto sul ponticello*, drawn over the bridge.

Trauer, mit (G.) With sadness.

trauernd (G.) Mourning, grieving.

träumerisch (G.) Dreamy. Also, **traumhaft.**

traurig (G.) Sad, mournful.

Traversflöte (G.) Same as FLAUTO TRAVERSO.

trb. (It.) Short for trombone(s).

tre (It.) Three, e.g., *a tre*, for three (parts).

tre corde (It.) Release the soft

(una corda) pedal. Also, **tutte le corde, t.c.**

treibend (G.) Hurrying, pressing on. Also, **treiben.**

trem. (It.) Short for TREMOLO.

tremblant (F.) In organs, the tremulant.

tremblement (F.) (1) Trembling, quivering. (2) Trill.

tremolando (It.) Quivering, trembling, rippling.

tremolo (It.) (1) A slight steady wavering of pitch. (2) In bowing, repeating the note very fast with the point of the bow. Also, **trem.**

trepidamente (It.) Anxious, fearful, trembling.

très (F.) Very much.

trg. (F.) Short for triangle.

trille (F.) Trill.

Triller (G.) Trill.

trillo (It., Sp.) Trill. Also, **tr.**

trinciante (It.) Cut up, separated, detached.

trino (Sp.) Trill.

Triole (G.) Triplet.

triomphant (F.) Triumphant, exultant, rejoicing.

trionfale (It.) Exultant, vicorious. Also, **trionfante.**

triple-croche (F.) Thirty-second note.

tristamente (It.) Wretchedly. Also, **tristo.**

triste (F., It., Sp.) Sad, mournful, grieving. Also (F.) **tristement,** (It.) **con tristezza, tristemente,** (Sp.) **con tristeza.**

triumphierend (G.) Triumphant, exultant.

trocken (G.) Dry, precise, without feeling.

trois (F.) Three.

tromba (It.) (1) Trumpet, bugle. (2) In organs, a chorus reed stop.

tromba piccolo (It.) Piccolo trumpet.

trombón (Sp.) Trombone.

Trommel (G.) Drum.

trompa (Sp.) French horn.

trompeta (Sp.) Trumpet.

Trompete (G.) Trumpet.

trompette (F.) (1) Trumpet. Also, **trompette à pistons,**

valve trumpet. (2) In organs, a loud chorus reed stop. Also, **French trumpet.**

trompette en chamade (F.) In organs, a chorus reed stop mounted in the front of the screen of the main organ or elsewhere, with the pipes in horizontal instead of vertical position. Also, **chamade, fan trumpet.**

trompette harmonique (F.) In organs, a very powerful 8-foot chorus reed stop.

tronco (It.) Cut short, abrupt.

trop (F.) Too, too much.

troppo (It.) Too, too much, e.g., *lento ma non troppo,* slow but not too slow.

trottinant, en (F.) At a regular rapid pace.

touche (F.) (1) Fingerboard (of violins, etc.). (2) Fret (of lutes, viols, etc.). (3) Key (of pianos, organs, etc.).

trüb (G.) Gloomy, sad.

tuba (1) (It., Sp.) Tuba, bass tuba. (2) (It.) Old name for trumpet. (3) (L.) Trumpet. (4) (It., L.) In organs, a name for various chorus reed stops with a firmer tone quality than the trompette or trumpet stops.

tuba magna (It., L.) In organs, a loud, brilliant chorus reed stop.

tuba mirabilis (It.) In organs, a very loud and intensely brass-like 8-foot tuba stop.

tumultueux, tumultueuse (F.) Stormy, noisy.

tumultuoso (It.) Noisy, agitated, an uproar.

turbulent (F.) Wild, stormy.

tutta, tutte, tutti (It.) (1) All total, e.g., *tutta forza*, with all (i.e., the most possible) force, *tutte unite*, all together. (2) Full orchestra or full chorus (as opposed to the soloist).

tutte le corde (It.) Same as TRE CORDE.

U

über (G.) Over, above, e.g., *R.H. über L.H.*, right hand (crossing) over the left hand.

Übergang (G.) Modulation, bridge.

übergehend (G.) Moving to, shading into, modulating.

übergreifen (G.) In keyboard music, to cross the hands,

e.g., *L.H. übergreifen*, cross left hand over right.

überlegen (G.) Lofty, superior.

überleiten (G.) Effect a transition.

übermässig (G.) Excessive, immoderate.

Übermut, mit (G.) With high spirits, merrily,, playfully. Also, **übermütig**.

überschwänglich (G.) Exuberantly.

übersetzen (G.) Cross over, e.g., *L.H. übersetzen*, cross left hand over (the right).

überströmend (G.) Overflowing, gushing, exultant.

übertrieben (G.) Exaggerated.

Überzeugung, mit (G.) With conviction.

übrigen, die (G.) The rest, others (as opposed to the soloist).

u.c. (It.) Short for UNA CORDA.

udibile (It.) Audible.

uguale (It.) Equal, uniform, the same.

uguaglianza, con perfetta (It.) Perfectly even, perfectly uniform.

ugualmente (It.) Equally, the same as, nevertheless.

ultima, ultimo (It.) The last.

um (G.) About, around, for, because of, e.g., *um ein geringes langsamer*, a little slower.

umore, con (It.) With humor, with wit.

un, une (F.) A, one.

un, una, uno (It.) A, one.

una corda (It.) Soft pedal. Also, u.c.

unaufdringlich (G.) Undemonstrative, unemphasized, colorless.

unaussprechbarem Entzücken, mit (G.) With unspeakable delight.

und (G.) And.

unda maris (L.) In organs, an undulating 8-foot stop made up of one or two ranks of pipes tuned slightly sharp or flat (if two ranks, one normal and one flat, or one sharp and one flat).

ungebunden (G.) Unrestrained, free.

ungeduldig (G.) Impatient. Also, mit Ungeduld.

ungefähr (G.) Approximate, approximately.

ungehemmt (G.) Unbounded, e.g., *mit ungehemmtem Entzücken*, with unbounded delight.

ungemein (G.) Extraordinarily, deeply, very.

ungestüm (G.) Violent, impetuous.

unhörbar (G.) Inaudible.

uni, unis (F.) Together, in unison.

uniforme (F.) Even, steady, regular.

unisono (It.) In unison, usually following a DIVISI section. Also, all' unisono, unis., uniti.

unmerklich (G.) Imperceptible.

unmutig (G.) Ill-humored, petulant, annoyed.

unregelmässig (G.) Uneven, irregular.

unrhytmisch (G.) Irregular, uneven.

unruhig (G.) Restless.

unschuldig (G.) Innocent.

unstät (G.) Unsteady, restless, aimless.

unten (G.) Below, under, underneath. Also, **unter.**

Untersatz (G.) In organs, same as SOUBASSE.

unterstützend (G.) Supporting.

üppig (G.) Rich, full, lush.

urlando (It.) Howling, shouting, shrieking.

ursprünglich (G.) Original, e.g., *ursprüngliches Tempo*, original tempo.

ut (F.) Same as DO, e.g., *trompette en ut*, C trumpet.

V

va (It.) Go, go on.

vagamente (It.) Wandering, straying, drifting.

vagaroso (Sp.) Wandering, flitting.

vaghezza, con (It.) (1) With charm, gracefully. (2) Obsolete name for ornament.

vaghissimo (It.) Very vague, very uncertain.

vago (It.) Vague, uncertain.

vague (F.) (1) Vague, indef-

inite. (2) A wave or billow, a surge.

valeur (F.) Time value.

valeurs irrationelles (F.) Unequal time values.

valore (It.) Time value, e.g., *doppio valore*, twice the previous time value (twice as slow).

vals (Sp.) Waltz.

valse (F.) Waltz.

valzer (It.) Waltz.

vaporeux (F.) Airy, vague.

vaporoso (It.) Very light, airy, transparent.

variante (F., It.) A different version.

variazione (It.) Variation. Also, **var.**

vaut (F.) Is equivalent to, e.g., ♩ *vaut la* ♪ *du début*, a quarter note is equivalent to the eighth note of the beginning.

veemente (It.) Intense, passionate.

véhémente (F.) Ardent, impetuous, emphatic.

velato (It.) Veiled, subdued.

vellutato (It.) Velvety, very smooth.

veloce (It.) Quite fast. Also, **velocemente, con velocità,** (F.) **véloce.**

veloz (Sp.) Fast.

vent, comme le (F.) Like the wind, light, airy.

verachtungsvoll (G.) Contemptuous, scornful.

Verbeugung, mit einer (G.) With a bow or curtsey.

verbreitern (G.) Broaden, similar to LARGO or LARGANDO.

verdianamente (It.) In the style of Verdi. Also, **verdiano.**

verdichten (G.) To condense, to speed up.

verdriesslich (G.) Peevish, vexed, depressed.

verdrossen (G.) Peevish, fretful, listless.

vergnügt (G.) Cheerful, merry.

verhallend (G.) Fading away.

verhaltener Stimme, mit (G.) In a low voice, in an undertone.

verhauchen (G.) (1) Exhale. (2) Dying away, with one's last breath.

verhauchend, ganz (G.) Expiring, dying away.

verhetzt (G.) Incited, aroused.

verinnerlicht (G.) Deepened, more intense, introspective.

verklärt (G.) Bright, radiant, transfigured.

verklingen (G.) To fade away. Also, **verklingend.**

verlangsamen (G.) To slow down.

verlassen (G.) To leave, to abandon.

verlierend (G.) Fading away.

verloren (G.) Hopeless, forlorn.

verlöschen (G.) Fade away, extinguish.

verrinend (G.) Becoming softer, dying away.

Verschiebung (G.) Soft pedal.

verschleiert (G.) Veiled, muffled.

verschwindend (G.) Disappearing, fading away.

versetzen (G.) To transpose.

versonnen (G.) Deeply thoughtful.

Verständnis, mit (G.) With insight, perceptively.

verstärken (G.) To swell, to become louder.

versunken (G.) Absorbed, preoccupied.

vertige, en un (F.) Dizzy, fast. Also, **vertigineux.**

vertiginoso (It.) Dizzily, very fast.

verträumt (G.) Dreamy.

Verwandlung (G.) (1) Change, transformation. (2) Change of scene.

verweilend (G.) Delaying, slowing down, becoming broader.

verzögernd (G.) Delaying, holding back, retarding.

verzückt (G.) Ecstatic, enraptured.

verzweifelt (G.) Despairing. Also, **verzweiflungsvoll.**

vez, à la (Sp.) At the same time.

vezzoso (It.) Graceful, charming.

via (It.) Away, remove, e.g., *via le sordini*, remove the mutes.

vibrador (Sp.) Same as VIBRATO (1).

vibrant (F.) (1) Vibrating, sounding. (2) A vibrato.

vibrante (1) (It.) Forceful, vigorous. Also, **vibrando.** (2) (Sp.) Vibrating, trembling.

vibrar (Port.) To sound.

vibratissimo (It.) (1) Trembling, very agitated. (2) With a great deal of VIBRATO (1).

vibrato (It.) (1) Pulsation of musical sound, on stringed instruments produced by rapid rocking of finger stopping the string. (2) Reverberating, resounding, ringing.

vibrer, laissez (F.) Continue to sound (do not mute or damp).

vibrieren lassen (G.) Continue to sound (i.e., do not mute or damp).

vicino (It.) Nearby, close.

vidalita (Sp.) A mournful love song.

vide (1) (F.) Open, e.g., *à vide*, open string. (2) (L.) See, indicating that the performer omit the notes between *vi-* and *-de*.

viel (G.) Much, a lot of, e.g., *mit viel Schwung*, with a lot of verve.

vieppiù (It.) Much more. Also, viepiù.

vier (G.) Four.

vierteilig (G.) Four-part.

Viertel (G.) Quarter note.

Viertelbewegung (G.) Literally, quarter-note rhythm, 4/4 time.

Vierundsechzigstel (G.) Sixty-fourth note.

vif (F.) Lively, animated. Also, vivement.

vigoroso (It.) Vigorously, boldly, energetically. Also, con vigore.

vigoureusement (F.) Energetic, forceful.

viol, viola (Sp.) Viola.

viola d'amore (It.) (1) An older instrument of the violin group. (2) In organs, a soft string stop.

viole (F.) Viol.

viole à pavillon (F.) In organs, a string stop of unusually bright but delicate tone.

viole conique (F.) In organs, an 8-foot string stop resembling the tone of a soft violin. Also, viole sordine, (It.) violino sordo.

viole d'orchestre (F.) In organs, an important string stop. Also, orchestral violin, violin.

violent (F.) Strong, forceful.

violento (Sp.) Impulsive, furious.

violenza, colla (It.) Vehemently, with force.

violetta (It.) In organs, a loud brilliant string stop.

violín (Sp.) Violin.

violino (It.) Violin.

violino da spalla (It.) Concertmaster.

violon (F.) Violin.

violón (Sp.) Double bass.

violoncelle (F.) Cello.

violoncello (It.) (1) Cello. (2) In organs, an important string stop with the tone of the orchestral cello. Also, cello.

violoncelo (Sp.) Cello.

violone (It.) (1) Contrabass viol. (2) In organs, same as CONTRA VIOLONE.

virtuoso (It.) Brilliant, technically very difficult.

visionär (G.) Visionary.

visionario (It.) Visionary.

vista, a (It.) At sight, sight-reading. Also, **a prima vista.**

vita, più (It.) Livelier, more animated.

vite (F.) Fast, rapid. Also, **vitement, vitesse.**

viv (It.) Short for VIVACE.

vivace (It.) A lively, brisk tempo, somewhat faster than ALLEGRO.

vivement (F.) Same as VIF.

vivezza, con (It.) Lively, brisk, animated.

vivido (It.) Lively, vigorous.

vivo (Sp.) Lively, intense.

vni. (It.) Short for violins.

voce (It.) Voice or voice-part. Also, (pl.) **voci,** e.g., *a due voci,* for two voices (parts).

voglia, con (It.) Longingly, eagerly.

voilé (F.) Also, **voilée.** (1) Veiled, subdued. (2) In singing, a husky tone.

voix (F.) Voice or voice-part.

voix blanche (F.) A light pure tone, with relatively few overtones.

voix céleste (F.) In organs, an 8-foot string stop of undulating tone, usually made up of two ranks of salicional pipes, one tuned normal and the other slightly sharp or slightly flat. Also, **céleste, vox céleste.**

voix humane (F.) In organs, same as VOX HUMANA.

voix intérieure (F.) Inner voice-part.

volando (It.) Flying, skimming rapidly.

volante (It.) Rushing, rapid.

volata (It.) A run or rapid passage.

volée, à toute (F.) Vibrating fully.

volgare (It.) Coarse, unrefined, common, popular.

volgare, con (It.) In the vernacular.

Volkslied (G.) Folksong.

Volkston, im (G.) Colloquially, popular, like a folksong.

volkstümlich (G.) Also, **volksthümlich.** Like a folksong or popular song.

voll (G.) Full, fully, completely.

vollem Ton, mit (G.) With a full tone. Also, **volltönend.**

vollständig (G.) Completely, wholly. Also, **vollkommen.**

volonté, à (F.) Freely, at the performer's discretion.

volta (It.) Time, e.g., *prima volta*, first time. Also, (pl.) **volte,** e.g., *due volte*, twice.

volteggiando (It.) Crossing hands (on the keyboard).

volti subito (It.) Turn the page quickly. Also, **v.s.**

volubile (F.) Fluent, flowing, rapid. Also, **volubilmente.**

volubilità, con (It.) Fickle, highly changeable, inconstant.

volupté, avec (F.) Full, rich, luxurious.

voluttuoso (It.) Luxuriously, sensuously.

vom (G.) From the, e.g., *vom Anfang*, from the beginning.

von (G.) From, e.g., *von fern*, from a distance.

vontade, a (Port.) At the performer's discretion.

vor (G.) Before, in front of, previous to.

voran (G.) (1) Before, ahead, in front. (2) Go on, continue.

vorangehen (G.) Preceding, leading, continuing.

vorbereiten (G.) To prepare in advance (with regard to organ stops, etc.).

Vorhang (G.) Curtain (of stage), e.g., *Vorhang auf*, raise the curtain.

vorher (G.) Before, previously.

vorig, vorige, voriger (G.) Former, previous, foregoing, e.g., *voriger Satz*, previous movement.

vor sich hin (G.) In front of one, forward.

Vortrag (G.) Style of delivery, execution, e.g., *frei im Vortrag*, in a free style.

vorwärts (G.) Go on, continue without pause, faster. Also, **vorwärtsgehen.**

vorwurfsvoll (G.) Reproachful.

vorzutragen (G.) To perform, to present.

vox (L.) Voice or voice-part.

vox acuta (L.) In organs, same as ACUTA.

vox angelica (L.) In organs, an 8-foot stop that represents the softest single rank of pipes.

vox céleste (L. + F.) Same as VOIX CÉLESTE.

vox gravissima (L. + It.) In organs, same as GRAVISSIMA.

vox humana (L. + It.) In organs, an important reed stop. Also, **Menschenstimme, voix humaine.**

vox mystica (L.) In organs, the softest reed stop.

voz (Sp.) Voice or voice-part.

v.s. (It.) Short for VOLTI SUBITO.

vuota (It.) Open, e.g., *corda vuota*, open string.

W

wachsend (G.) Growing louder.

wählerisch (G.) Fastidious, dainty, choosy.

Waldflöte (G.) In organs, an open, moderately loud flute stop. Also, **Feldflöte,** (L.) **tibia**

sylvestris.

Waldhorn (G.) In organs, a reed stop designed to sound like a hunting horn. Also (F.) **cor de chasse,** (It.) **corno di caccia, hunting horn.**

wallend (G.) Boiling, simmering.

Walzer (G.) Waltz.

Walzerzeitmass (G.) Waltz time.

Wärme, mit (G.) With warmth, with feeling.

wechselnd (G.) Changing, e.g., *in wechselndem Tempo,* in changing tempo.

weg (G.) Away, off, e.g., *Dämpfer weg,* without mute.

Weh, mit (G.) With pain, lamenting.

wehmütig (G.) Sad, melancholy.

weich (G.) Soft, gentle.

weichflüssig (G.) Sweetly flowing.

weihevoll (G.) Worshipful, solemn. Also, **mit Weihe.**

weinerlich (G.) Weepy, tearful. Also, **weinend.**

weiterklingen (G.) Continuing to sound.

weltentrückt (G.) Solitary,
withdrawn.

wenig (G.) Little.

weniger (G.) Less.

werden (G.) To become, e.g.,
leise werden, become soft.

wesentlich (G.) (1) Funda-
mental, basic. (2) Chiefly,
essentially.

wie (G.) As, e.g., *wie vorher*, as
before, *wie zu Beginn*, as in
the beginning.

wieder (G.) Again.

Wiederholung (G.) Repeat.

wiegend (G.) Rocking, swaying
rhythmically.

wild (G.) Tumultuous, passionate.

wirbelnd (G.) (1) Warbling. (2)
Sounding a drumroll.

womöglich (G.) If possible.

wuchtig (G.) Ponderous, slow,
emphatic.

wühlend (G.) Violent.

würdig (G.) Stately, dignified.
Also, **mit Würde.**

wütend (G.) Furious, enraged.

X Y Z

xilófono (Sp.) Xylophone.

y (Sp.) And.

zaghaft (G.) Shy, timid,
wavering.

zänkisch (G.) Quarrelsome,
scolding.

zart (G.) Tender, delicate, soft.
Also, **mit Zartheit, zärtlich.**

Zartflöte (G.) In organs, an
open flute stop of subdued
tone.

Zauberflöte (G.) In organs, a
stopped flute stop, moderately
soft and of very clear tone.

zeffiroso (It.) Very light and
airy.

Zeit (G.) (1) Time, a pause. (2)
Tempo.

Zeit lassen (G.) (1) Perform
freely (with regard to tempo),
do not rush. (2) Allow for a
pause.

Zeitmass (G.) Tempo.

zeloso (It.) Fervently, ardently.

ziemlich (G.) Rather, quite,
e.g., *ziemlich schnell*, quite fast.

zierlich (G.) Dainty, graceful, elegant.

Zimbel (G.) (1) Cymbal. (2) In organs, a brilliant mixture stop made up of open metal foundation pipes. Also, **cymbal.**

Zimbelflöte (G.) In organs, same as CAMPANA (3).

Zink (G.) (1) The obsolete cornett (wind instrument). (2) In organs, a pedal reed stop.

zitternd (G.) Trembling.

zögernd (G.) Hesitating, holding back.

zornig (G.) Angry.

zu (G.) (1) To. (2) Too, e.g., *nicht zu langsam*, not too slow.

zufrieden (G.) Satisfied, contented, peaceful.

zügig (G.) Spirited, fiery.

zum (G.) To the, e.g., *bis zum Schluss*, to the end.

zunehmend (G.) (1) Increasing, e.g., *mit zunehmender Leidenschaft*, with increasing passion. (2) Growing louder.

Zungenschlag (G.) Tonguing.

zurückhalten (G.) To hold back, to slow down. Also, **zurückhaltend.**

zurückkehrend (G.) Returning.

zurücknehmen (G.) To withdraw.

zurücksinkend (G.) Falling back, relapsing.

zurücktreten (G.) To retreat, to become softer.

zusammen (G.) Together.

zuversichtlich (G.) Confident, hopeful.

zuvor, als (G.) As before.

zwanglos (G.) Unconstrained, free.

zwei (G.) Two.

zweite (G.) Second, e.g., *zweite Fassung*, second version.

zweiteilig (G.) Two-part.

Zweiunddreisigstel (G.) Thirty-second note.

zwischen (G.) Between.

Zwischenspiel (G.) Interlude, intermezzo.

Zwischenvorhang (G.) Drop curtain.

Vowels and diphthongs
a (arte) as in art, father
ai (aiuto) as in file
ao (Paolo) as in foul
au (fausto) as in foul
e (tre) as in pen
i before a consonant (fine) as in keep, mean
i before a vowel (piano, pieno, più) as in yes, opinion
o (come) as in topic
u (duro, tutti) as in poor, too

Consonants and consonant combinations
c before a, o, u (caro, con, culto) as in can
c, cc before e, i (cento, cima, cuccina) as in chief
ch (che) as in can
g before a, o, u (gaio, goffo, gusto) as in get
g before e, i (gentile, gioco) as in general
gg before e, i (leggere, leggio) as in courage
gh before e, i (ghezzo, ghiaccio) as in guilt
gl before a, e, o, u (glaciale, glotta) as in gleam
gl before i (gli) as in brilliant
gn (legno) as opinion
h (hai) as in honor (always silent).
qu (questo) as in question
s (secco) as in English (sense) except when between two vowels
    (mese), then soft as in rose
sc before e, i (scena, scienzia) as in shade
z, zz may be either hard (zio), as in flotsam, or soft (canzona), as
    in zone

Stress
The primary accent is usually on the next-to-last syllable or on
the final vowel where it bears a written accent (città), but there are
numerous exceptions.

Vowels and diphthongs

A vowel is long when followed by a single consonant (usually), when doubled, or when followed by the letter **h**. A vowel is short when followed by more than one consonant, and, in some short words, when followed by a single consonant.

long **a, aa, ah** (Vater, Haare, Hahn) as in father
short **a** (Haft) as in but
ai, ay (Mai, Mayer) as in my
au (laut) as in out
long **ä, äh** (Mädchen, fähig) as in fate
short **ä** (Kälte) as belt, let
äu (Fräulein) as in toil
long **e, ee, eh** (Segel, Seele, Sehnsucht) as in gay, pain
short **e** (Bett) as in yet
e in unaccented syllables (Glocke) as in open, upon
ei, ey (mein, Meyer) as in line
er (fertig) as in air, bare
er in unaccented syllables (Diener) as in butter
eu (heulen) as in oil
long **i, ie, ih** (hin, schief, ihnen) as in feel, lean
short **i** (mit, binden) as in it
long **o, oh, oo** (wo, Hohn, Boot) as in quote, boat
short **o** (kommen) pronounced halfway between but and rod
long **ö, öh** (böse, Höhle) similar to hurt or her but longer
short **ö** (Hölle) similar to unaccented fetter but shorter.
long **u, uh** (gut, Schuh) as in loot
short **u** (und) as in foot, put
long **ü, üh** (trüb, Mühe) similar to saying, with lips shaped for **oo**, the sound **ee** as in keep
short **ü, y** (Glück, Typus) similar to saying, with lips shaped for **oo**, the sound of **i** as in lip

Consonants and consonant combinations

b (baden) as in bath, except at end of word (gab), then pronounced as p, as in gap
c before e, ä, i, y (Celsius) as in flotsam

118

ch after a, o, u, au (auch, Tuch) pronounced by forcing the
    breath between tongue and uvula
ch after ei, eu, i (ich, weich) similar to the **h** in whispering huge
ch in words of Greek origin (Chor) as in **ch**orus
d (da) as in date, except at end of word (Kind), then pronounced
    as **t**, as in cat
g before vowels (Gabel, gut) as in **g**ate, **g**ive
g at end of word (Tag) pronounced as **k**, as in tac**k**
g in the closing syllables ig, igst, igt (wenig) is pronounced as a
    ch after ei, eu, i (see above)
j (jung) as in yes
kn (Knie) pronounced by sounding both **k** and **n** in succession.
pf (Pfund) pronounced by sounding both **p** and **f** in succession.
ph (Phantasie) as in **ph**onic
ps (Psalmodie) pronounced by sounding both **p** and **s**
qu (Quelle) pronounced by sounding first **k** and then **v**
s at beginning of word or syllable (sagen, rasieren) as in rise, zero
s at end of word or syllable (das, Kasse) as in sun, mass
sch (schön) as in **sh**ine
sp at beginning of word or syllable (Sprache) pronounced by
    sounding first **sh** and then **p**
ss, sz (gross, Szene) as in sun
st at beginning of word or syllable (stets) pronounced by sounding
    first **sh** and then **t**
th (Thema) as in take
tz (sitzen) as in flotsam
v (von) as in father
w (wo) as in very
z (zu) as in flotsam, tsar

Stress

The primary accent falls on the stem syllable, usually the first
syllable. In words compounded with syllables before the stem
(prefixes) the prefix is accented unless it is one of the following,
which are never accented: be-, emp-, ent-, er-, ge-, ver-, zer-. In
words ending with -ei the accent falls on the last syllable.

French Pronunciation

Vowels and Diphthongs

short **a** (patte) midway between the a in father and cat
long **a, â** (tard, âme) as in father
ai (lait) as in debt
an (dans) as in **aw**ning
au (faux) as in **go**
é (clé) as in fate but more open
è, ê (élève, même) as in debt but longer
e in unaccented syllables (refrain) as in open, again
eau (beau) as in **go**
ei (feindre) as in debt
en (enfin) as in **aw**ning
short **eu** (neveu) similar to saying, with lips shaped to sound **oh**,
    the sound of **e** in bed
long **eu** (nerveuse) similar to saying, with lips shaped to sound **oh**,
    the sound of **a** in ale
euil (feuille) similar to saying, in rapid succession, the long **eu**
    (see above) and **ee**
eur (faveur) as in **purr** but longer
long **i, î** (cri, intîme) as in **beef**
short **i** (ville, dire) as in **mere**
in (enfin) as in **fan** but more nasalized
short **o** (voler) similar to folly but shorter
long **ô** (rôle) similar to **dole**
oe (oeuf) same as short **eu**
oi (bois) as in **wander**
on (bonbon) similar to saying **dong** but with a long **o** (as in
    phone) and with the g nasalized
short **ou** (bourse) as in **poor**
long **ou** (tout) as in **tool**
short **u** (une) similar to saying with lips shaped to say **oo**, the
    sound of **i** as in tip
long **u** (rue, salut) similar to saying, with lips shaped to say **oo**,
    the sound of **ee** as in keep
ui (huit) similar to saying, in rapid succession, **oo-ee**
uin (juin) similar to saying, in rapid succession, **oo-an**
un (défunt) similar to saying, in rapid succession, **oh-an**

Consonants and consonant combinations
c before a, o, u (carte, coquette, cul) as in cake
c before e, i (cette, ciel) as in salad
ch (charge) as in shall
g before a, o, u (galant, gout, guide) as in get
g before e, i (gentil, gilet) as in gentle but softer, like the zh
      sound in vision
gn (agneau, soigné) similar to the ny sound in annual
h (hacher) always silent, as in honor
j (juste) like the zh sound in vision, mirage
qu (qualité) as in canter
s (sec) as in salad, except when between two vowels (raser), then
      soft as in rise
v (vif) as in village
w (wagon) as in village
x at the end of words may be silent (aux) or sounded (six) as in
      geese

Liaison
When a word begins with a vowel or with a mute h, in most cases it is joined with the last consonant of the preceding word, even when that consonant is followed by a mute e. In such instances the final consonant is pronounced as though it were the first letter of the second word, as in **avec elle**, pronounced as ah-vek-el.

Stress
Unlike English, Italian, and German, in French the primary accent tends to fall on the last syllable.

Notes and Rests

Whole note	![whole note]	Whole rest	—
Half note		Half rest	—
Quarter note		Quarter rest	}
Eighth note		Eighth rest	7
16th note		16th rest	⅞
32nd note		32nd rest	⅞
64th note		64th rest	⅞

Clefs

Treble clef (G clef)

Bass clef (F clef)

middle C

Tenor clef (C clef)   Alto clef (C clef)

middle C

Accidentals

♯	Sharp	Raises pitch one half tone within measure.
♭	Flat	Lowers pitch one half tone within measure.
𝄪	Double sharp	Raises pitch two half tones within measure.
𝄫	Double flat	Lowers pitch two half tones within measure.
♮	Natural	Cancels previous sharp or flat appearing within measure or indicated by key signature.

Key Signatures

Position of each accidental on the staff shows which note is affected, e.g., F in G major/E minor, F and C in D major/B minor, etc.

Intervals

Brackets show enharmonic intervals, identical on keyboard.

Ornaments and Signs

Accented note

Acciaccatura

Written *Played*

Appoggiatura (long)

Written *Played*

Arpeggio

Written *Played*

Détaché

Down-bow ⊓ **Up-bow** V

Dynamic changes

Louder Softer Louder, then softer

Grace note (short appoggiatura)

Louré

Martelé

Mordent **Inverted mordent**

Written Played Written Played

Double mordent

Written Played

Nachschlag

Written Played

Pause (Fermata) ⌢

Piqué (or Portato)

Portamento

Repeat

Written Played

Written Played

Written Played

Slur (or Legato)

Staccato Accented staccato

Tie

Written Played

Tremolo

Bowed Fingered Keyboard

Trill

Written Played (after Beethoven)

Written Played
(17th - 18th C.) (up to Beethoven)

Turn

Written Played

Inverted turn

Written Played

ABOUT THE AUTHOR

CHRISTINE AMMER, a lexicographer, was born in Vienna, is a graduate of Swarthmore College, and speaks several languages. She is the author of *The Harper Dictionary of Music*, a popular reference work for two decades, and *Unsung: A History of Women in American Music*, as well as reference books in other fields. In recent years she has written and lectured widely about the role of women musicians and composers. She is a member of the Sonneck Society and an associate of American Women Composers and the International League of Women Composers.

Foreign Languages for Singers

DICTION
By JOHN MORIARTY

E. C. Schirmer
Catalog No. 650

A comprehensive guide to the pronunciation of Italian, French, Ecclesiastical Latin, and German.

"...a model of completeness, clarity and organization...this unique and valuable reference tool should find a permanent place in the collections of singers, teachers of singing and choral conductors." —*NATS Bulletin*

"Herein, three common hazards to singers (Italian, French and German) are dealt with in concise terms, using the standard international phonetic alphabet, and are made lucid by a thorough comparison to equivalent sounds in English. Even the simplest among us cannot but benefit from the serious application of this amassment of material. My only regret is that so many of us had to learn the hard and long way what is available here."
—*Professor Margaret Harshaw, Indiana University*

Now firmly established as the classic instruction and reference book for singing foreign languages, this 275-page volume carefully describes the physical process of forming vowels and consonant sounds, compares them language by language, and demonstrates them in a series of systematic exercises. Part II sets forth the rules of stage pronunciation for each language, with specific notes on pitfalls common to American singers.